Tulcidious
Ascension to Love & Wisdom

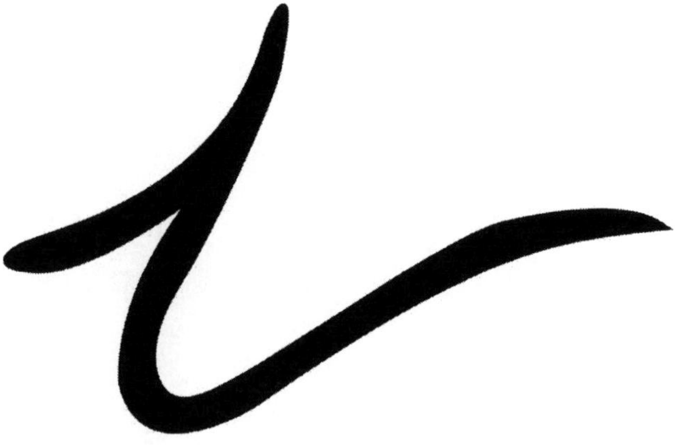

Tulcidious
Ascension to Love & Wisdom

A Vocabulary for Conscious Human Thought

Michael R. Meng, JD

Tulcidious
Ascension to Love & Wisdom

A Vocabulary for Conscious Human Thought

Michael R. Meng, JD

This is the 20th year edition of a work required into existence in 1999 & first published in 2000. It is the instruction manual for a set of wooden objects you will find described and discussed here. The next image you will see within shows their faces.

ISBN: 9798691084027
TLW

**For Every Woman Who Has
Ever Lived**

and the affirmation of humanity's successful
relationship with an ever less violent
and more symbiotic world.

READ THIS FIRST

It could not possibly be obvious from a first glance at twenty-nine simple hand-drawn symbols that they can serve as an introductory pathway to understanding all existence. This book will offer you the possibility of seeing that pathway by identifying a three-part division among the general concepts of Creativity, Survival Skills, and the Birth of Individuality, as those ideas occur in human thinking. It is the brash and basic claim of this short book that the twenty-nine distinctions identified here in those three groups can provide a legitimate means for grasping and managing your individual experience of the whole of human thinking.

That such abilities might be possible to each of us may be something you have never considered. Whether you can accept these claims or not and whether or not you may hold the substantive gifts of the proposed distinctions will unfold only after you allow yourself to know the simple meaning of these twenty-nine symbolic representations. Sharing that knowledge is the first purpose of this book.

Those twenty-nine ideas and the symbolic representations of them are collectively referred to as "Tulcidious" and individually as "Tules." The first "u" in Tulcidious is pronounced like the "oo" in wool. "Tule" is pronounced like "tool."

For the easiest, most immediate introduction, the simple key to their meanings is found in the table of Contents following this section.

Collectively Tulcidious is a representational mechanism for a curriculum of thought founded in the best of human nature: the caring we each hold for our nearest and dearest. That "curriculum of thought" is a group of ideas gathered together as a vocabulary for the specific purpose of advancing the level of your own self-awareness.

Examining one's personal manner of being with these Tules helps supply the freedom of choice to remove or control those impacts of culture and early life experience which can impair who we really are.

This collection of twenty-nine ideas is also the result of a private, independent exploration into the nature and history of all human existence and intelligence as best we can know them both, and it constitutes a vast simplification.

The three questions at the heart of that exploration were "How did all this get started?" "Where does humanity stand now?" and "How can our way from here on be both aided and eased?" Tulcidious supplies a doorway to continually identifying your own most personally supportive responses to all three of these questions. The second purpose of this book is to make visible the way the Tules help to unfold meaning in our lives and how to take advantage of them.

The Tules will provide a sense of understanding and organization around the multitude of thinking events that take place for you every day. Although feelings are only occasionally mentioned specifically in the text, the Tules will also help you more fully recognize and actualize the gifts within your own feeling states. They help to ease fear and confusion in daily life.

As an explanation of the ideas represented by the individual Tules, this book is merely a beginning. You will fulfill your understanding of the Tules for yourself. In the same way that an alphabet of language provides the beginning means to make written communication possible, the Tules identify an organized and easily multi-dimensional starting place limited only by the furthest reaches of human imagination and experience. For these reasons you may notice an intentionally brief, raw, and bare, even limited quality to what you find here. The Tules are a starting place.

The "Compendium" section is the place where the specific meaning of each individual Tule is explained. There are three distinct groups, called Full Presence (your life in creativity), The Lifeboat (essentials of survival), and The Vibrations of the Earth (the birth of individuality). Each of the three groups is explained more fully at the beginning of its section.

You will notice that the three groups of Tules can be distinguished by their shapes. The Full Presence Tules are round. There are nine Lifeboat Tules and they are each nine-sided. There are seven Vibrations Tules and they are each seven-sided.

You will also quickly realize that the individual explanations in the Compendium are, for the most part, quite straightforward and simple. However, go slow. The Tules are intended to be a comprehensive source of food for thought. The text offers many examples intended to welcome both your thoughts about those examples and your reactions to the questions around how the ideas presented fit in your daily life. As you get to know them, do so as gradually as necessary to allow yourself to be guided by your own thoughts and feelings.

It is recommended that you refer to the Compendium entries in whatever order you are moved to, at first by your curiosity about the symbols. Finally, be sure to read the entire book so that you can achieve a responsible competence in your use of the Tules.

Contents

Contents

Contents

Introduction

Tulcidious is an identified collection of contextual concepts or themes, all common in human thinking, offered to supply an easy representational means for you to intentionally own an ever-larger authority over your experience of daily life. In that sense they are tools for life. This book is their instruction manual. Think of each Tule as a container for a group of ideas or a concept that begins with a relatively simple name, such as Trust or Exploration, and identifies a major component within your human awareness.

Each Tule is a doorway into an entirely distinct realm of thought within the idea defined by its name. The Tules provide an intentionally broad invitation to the application of your own intuition which will grow as you expand your experience of using them. You will ultimately define your own understanding of the Tules, yet there is a right way to begin. Allow yourself to be guided by what you read here in order to establish your initial sense of the Tules and their individual meanings.

The Tules are designed specifically to aid your growth by making you aware of natural processes already taking place within your awareness. They will advance the level at which you enjoy life by awakening you to the relationship between your activities and your Nature. This helps make it possible for you to bring the two more successfully in line with each other.

Write in this book freely, as you see fit.

The Vibrations of the Earth~ the birth of individuality.

Tulcidious is divided into three distinct groups, identified by the symbols on the back of each Tule. The foundational group of seven Tules (presented last in the text) is called "The Vibrations of the

Earth." Each Tule in this group shows an easily recognizable image of a tree on its reverse. If you can consider our Earth to be a living "being" with a consciousness of its own (distinct in its Nature and apart from our human forms of consciousness), then you will be able to appreciate the conception that the Vibrations Tules depict the ordered progression of stages in awareness which the Earth experienced as it came into existence. The Tules depict the idea that this experiential conception is meaningfully relatable to human consciousness.

Full Presence~ states of being, a home for creativity.

The first group, which contains thirteen Tules, is the "Full Presence" group. Each of these Tules displays on its reverse side the face of the Self, as you see here. Think of this as your own face. One of these Tules

displays that face on both sides. This one, called "Full Presence," is the heart of all the Tules. The remaining twelve in the group depict individual "states of being," each of which can be considered a part of your moment-by-moment daily way of life. If you can accept that idea, then these twelve states of being can also be described as one source in human life for all our naturally creative ways.

The Lifeboat~ elemental survival skills.

 The third group, of nine Tules, is "The Lifeboat." The back sides of these Tules show an image of a Lifeboat, empty and still at sea. The Lifeboat Tules represent the nine major skills humans have used throughout our long history in the struggle mainly to survive the hostile elements of the planet.

It is easy to become confused in our daily human lives. It is also easy to think that there is some pre-determined right way to deal with everything that you are confronted by in your life. It is true that you're likely to commonly be beset by other people, as well as a sense of domination rising from the culture you live in, telling you (directly or otherwise) some 'right way' to deal with anything you meet. The younger you are the more likely this is. And if there is a right way to deal with your life, that is honestly and intentionally while caring, all as well as you are personally and individually able.

It becomes understandable that you might ask: "Well then, if that's so, how am I supposed to think I'm getting there?" Clearing your mind of confusion will help. If you gain clarity about what's taking place in your mind, you may find yourself more consciously in charge of the experience. Helping you do that is one of the major purposes of the Tules. Being more consciously in charge of what's taking place in your own mind will make it easier to relate to the other people you connect with in all aspects of your life.

> "Another major purpose of the Tules is to grow your personal sense of inner strength and competence."

Getting Started

One way to begin is by bringing some order to your set. If you find value in your experience of these Tules, you may want to give them a place of their own in your home apart from the book. For now, just give them enough room on a table or desk so you can spread them out as described here.

The reverse side of each Tule displays the image that identifies its group. A face for the Full Presence group, an empty Lifeboat for that group, and a mature tree for the Vibrations of the Earth group.

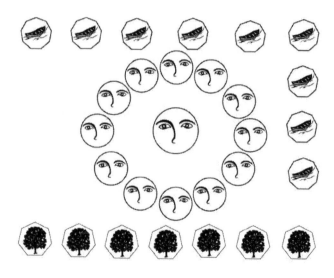

Now, with those images on bottom, spread out the Tules as shown in the next image, with their faces up~

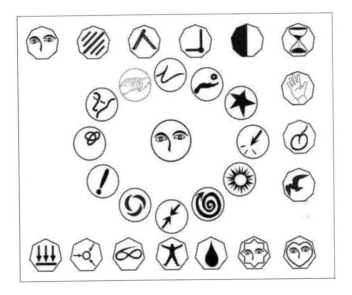

Arrange the Full Presence group in a circle, like the hours on a clock, beginning alphabetically at the one o-clock position. You may need to refer to the Compendium to match the names and symbols. Be sure to notice that the face of the Self appears in all three groups.

Spread out the Vibrations Tules below the circle to match the order shown in the layout display above, in a straight line from left to right. For the Lifeboat Tules, spread them out above the Full Presence Tules, in a line from left to right, in the order shown in the layout display above with six across the top, and the remaining three down the right side, below the sixth.

Full Presence

Next, begin to familiarize yourself more fully with their individual names, starting with the Full Presence group. In the layout image depicting their faces, the alphabetical progression begins at the one o-clock position with Blossoming, also known as Presentation. They are, in order:

> Blossoming, Presentation
> Declaration
> Discovery
> Expansion
> Exploration
> Focusing
> Meditation
> Recognition
> Refinement
> Rest
> Thanks
> Tulcidious.

Allow yourself to begin to memorize this list of names in that alphabetical order. One of the early enjoyable ways to notice the flash points in your sensate awareness is to practice identifying these twelve "states of being" by writing down their names or the symbols for each from memory, or by naming the Tules as you turn up the face of each and separating out the ones you can't name.

As you become familiar with doing that, look at what you are called to think about by the Tules whose names you were unable to remember. If, for example, you can't recall the symbol used to represent Declaration, maybe it's time to make more Declarations, or to work less at doing so, or to find out what Declarations are and start allowing yourself to understand in what way you are making Declarations at some level every moment. You are.

Keep in mind that there is no single, perfect right way to integrate this information. Memorization is suggested only as one common, familiar mechanism. The Full Presence Tules represent inherent states of being. The Vibrations Tules represent a foundational progression of experiences. The Lifeboat Tules represent innate survival skills. The Tules will introduce themselves. Let yourself begin with the Full Presence group by memorizing those twelve names in the alphabetical order given. If you are moved to do it, familiarize yourself more fully with the rest any way you like.

After you have laid the Tules out, allow yourself to think about priorities. The arrangement of the Full Presence Tules in the layout display, alphabetically and like the numbers on a clock, was set that way as an introduction. As you establish a basic understanding of their meanings, rearrange them in the way that seems the most meaningful to you now. Notice their relations. Notice which one seems most prominent to you and which one you want to think about the least. Notice what priority you might be moved to apply among them. Go slowly to respect the noticing.

The Tules are intended to serve you individually and privately. They are far more than a game. Your honesty with yourself is their lifeblood. Of course, you are free to share your experience of the Tules. If you find it difficult to speak honestly with others about what you see of your own life in the Tules, then be kind to yourself and refrain from making any effort to do so.

Next, turn the Tules over, mix them up completely (or close your eyes), and choose one. Admit how the idea presented by the one you chose speaks to you. Allow yourself to notice your emotional reaction to the effort you are making. If you are comfortable with them, you may begin to let the Tules contribute to your personal sense of purpose. Otherwise you will likely let them go. You may only gain a sense of their value as you explore and become more familiar with their individual meanings in the Compendium.

In this first intentional experience of being with the Tules, spend as much time as required to allow yourself to arrive at a completed feeling state you are willing to acknowledge, if only to yourself. When you do, that will be the end of your second meeting with the Tules. The first was when you saw them the first time. Your beginner status is now complete.

The Vibrations of the Earth

Moving on to the Vibrations, arrange these Tules in the order shown in the second layout image. In that image, the Vibrations are the seven Tules at the bottom of the display. From left to right, they are:

Gravity, A Wave Within
Unthinkable Pressure

Multitudes Beyond Imagination
Exposure
Insanity
Trust Yourself
Love Yourself.

If you can conceive of our Earth "totalistically" as a sentient being, then you may be able to understand this order as identifying a specific progression of experience that the Earth went through in the process of coming into its perhaps conscious existence. The Vibrations Tules depict a way of understanding the Earth's birth experience. Their meanings are described individually in the Compendium.

The Lifeboat

Among the Lifeboat Tules (at the top and right side in the layout display) the only important specific thing is that the first one comes first. Their names, in the order shown in the layout display, beginning at the left, are:

Presence for the Self
Integrity
Trust
Responsibility
Contrast
Time
Willingness
Ability
Freedom.

The Lifeboat Tules depict humanity's long struggle for survival and, with the Full Presence Tules, the opportunity to use our experience to surmount the limits we so frequently impose upon ourselves.

How Does a Tule Appear?

A Tule appears when you select it. Your selection of any of the Tules is an aspect of acceptance. Acceptance is an aspect of Willingness. Willingness is to have the mind favorably disposed to doing some specific thing, not refusing. The appearance of any Tule for you, then, begins when you are favorably disposed to allowing them collectively to have a useful presence or purpose in your life. That may have occurred when you chose to buy this book, or to accept it as a gift from someone else. That may be occurring now. You are the sole judge of this, though without at least that minimal level of acceptance on your part, they are meaningless.

If you have made it beyond this small, basic matter of acceptance, then the Tules and your understanding of their meanings will aid you in expanding an awareness of your own primarily thought-based functioning. They may also help you in ordering that functioning more successfully.

As you become familiar with the Tules and what they individually mean for you, beyond the basic explanations contained in this book, you may find consistencies. Allow yourself into all that this may unfold. Your expanded familiarity may also show you patterns in your functioning. Welcome what you see in this way and allow yourself to examine your feelings about the level of utility those patterned ways of functioning may hold. Allow the patterns and consistencies you find to help you look further, both into and around the relationships in your life.

Advancing your familiarity with the Tules may also cause you to find continually expanding intricacies. If an idea presented by a Tule becomes "old hat" for you, yet that Tule keeps appearing, it is an invitation to look for new levels of meaning. When this occurs, be sure to read the Compendium entry on that Tule again.

"Paradox reminds us that the larger the challenge, the simpler the solution."

Much of our attention is bound in denying such paths in thinking though they may hold the possibility of advancing ease in your personal experience.

The Basics of Using the Tules

These Tules are a way of addressing the question, "are you as fully engaged as you would like in the opportunity that life offers?"

Begin now again by turning them all face down, so that the backs are showing. Mix them up. Remember that the appearance of a Tule is your selection of it. Choose one. Read the full explanation of its meaning in the Compendium. Acknowledge for yourself what that Tule causes you to think or feel. Look first at the most prominent thought or feeling that comes to mind.

If you are with other people when you do this, and you notice a reluctance to be fully open about what a Tule carries you to in awareness, then it is best to use the Tules privately. One common stance in Trust will cause many to be cautious in what they choose to share with others. The Tules are primarily intended for private use, yet unless you live alone, it is likely you will want to discuss your experience of the Tules with others. When the novelty wears off, use the Tules privately.

Intuition, Honesty & Choice

Using the Tules consistently offers an opportunity lesson in honesty and intuition. In the realm of thought the Tules provide a natural way of applying your attention, arguably as fully as watching television or the experience of driving, though less mechanistic or debilitating than either. Once you are satisfied that you can understand and accept the attention required to use the Tules, let yourself consider the impact of two (or, as you may wish~ more) at once. Close your eyes, mix them up, choose two, and examine their meanings in the Compendium.

Remember, it is likely that you will want to come at the Tules with one or more of the specific challenges that you normally make individual choices about. It is a common human theme to seek outside support or affirmations for our actions to a greater or lesser degree. The Tules exist to splay out before you a way of identifying, understanding, and managing the prominent themes in your own thought. If you have some particularly difficult choice to make, the Tules may compel you to admit that fact though their purpose is to make you stop and think rather than to make your choices for you.

Yet the predictable may also be inevitable. See if you can smile around the following example, as it can help us see how entirely fluid our human ways are, how fully we tend to cover all the gray areas.

If you were to come to the Tules with some "Yes or No" question such as, "Should I date him?" or "Should

I take that job?" and you closed your eyes and randomly chose any two Tules (which is a perfectly acceptable way of doing that), you might come up with the Lifeboat Tule, Trust, and the Full Presence Tule, Exploration. Then how would you choose between the immediate messages, "Explore Trust" and "Trust Exploration?" They could seem to be contradicting each other in the face of your question.

If you were in a rush to have some such choice made for you by an outside force, it would be easy to be satisfied with whichever of those two simple answers seemed preferable in the moment, to supply the yes or no needed (if you do see two messages, the more accurate is the first that appeared). That's the predictable though, and the opportunity is instead to allow yourself a more intimate examination of the issue, rather than looking for a fast solution. The Tules exist to help you look at your choices, rather than to make them for you.

The fast solution may be all you need or want in the moment, and you will learn to use the Tules in the way you personally prefer and feel most comfortable with. Their continual invitation, however, is the challenge to look at any such questions with your fullest honesty, rather than quickly reaching for whatever some easy or comfortable answer may be. The only pitfall here would be the failure to make the choice for yourself. The Tules will serve more effectively to identify issues, rather than as a complex coin to flip.

In using the Tules guide yourself primarily by letting them merely suggest areas within your reality to examine.

You may quickly see that every opportunity you take to consider what the Tules offer includes the invitation to face and address the matters of how you define your own sense of intuition and how honest you are with yourself.

Remember that this process the Tules are intended to initiate in your life is a private one. The largest challenge you will find in the Tules is the choice to complete the reading of this entire book. The gifts of the Tules can become innately natural in your life when you complete this reading. The individual objects are meant to be simple reminders, like road signs, that you can easily use to return your attention to these consistent themes in your own awareness.

The varieties of possibility in thought that are offered through the perspective of these twenty-nine marking posts are beyond any counting, and for that reason very little specific direction is given here around the matter of how you will come to use them when they are no longer new. That's an intentional invitation to finding the best way for yourself. Intuitively.

Using your intuition is living in the truth about what you feel. Honesty is in part telling the truth about what you see. What you feel begins as accessible only to you. This means that in the realm of relationships, life will likely prove easier if we allow our sense of honesty to rule when it confronts our intuition. When honesty and intuition meet face to face while you are alone, let honesty enthrall your intuition. This will welcome more fully the presence and manner of your hearted being.

After understanding the basics of their individual meanings as explained in the Compendium, you are the sole judge of what the appearance of any Tule or combination means for you in any given moment. Also remain clear that the given moment is what matters. The appearance of the same one or two Tules tomorrow means a different thing than it does today. Let honesty and intuition be your sole guides.

Expanding Your Understanding and Use of the Tules

I.

The Tules are intended to depict the features of what may be called your emotional, sensate state. They represent fibers of thought and identify elements of your awareness. Natural human tendencies might cause some to wonder why only these twenty-nine concepts are represented as Tules. Prominent among concepts left out are Choice and Understanding. The reason for this might help you understand your own nature more fully. It will certainly help you understand the Tules more fully.

Choice is either a conscious methodological act or a neuro-psychological event. Understanding is a result. The aspects of humanness identified by the Tules are elements of thought and awareness. The Full Presence Tules identify states of being. They are not methodologies. They are not results. They are aspects of being that may be seen like common pathways within your Nature.

The Lifeboat Tules depict concepts that are abstract or generic ideas generalized from individual instances. The Vibrations Tules comprise highlights in a narrative, best efforts at transliterating distinct experiences.

II.

When some specific Tule appears, you may feel little connection to the description of its meaning found in the Compendium. This is normal.

These Tules are reminders which it is best to view as invitations, merely to consider the Compendium's offerings and ask yourself what they may mean for you today.

You are the only person who can define your relationship or experience with the Tules and what they offer in your life. Their offerings change every moment and are different for every person.

Also, if anyone else ever tests you on your understanding of the Tules or the Compendium's stated meanings for them, you may fairly see your tester as mis-using both you and the Tules. The Compendium is a starting place, intended to be firm, specific, defined, and certain. We all will fulfill its purpose most when we use the Tules to allow ourselves to expand, continually adding meaning, rather than limiting or constricting our understandings.

At the level of interaction, the Tules are food for continually expanding conversation connected to your specific life experiences. The only right way to use them is to begin.

III.

When you come to see yourself as "at home" with the Tules you may want to keep them spread out face up somewhere. After all, they are mainly reminders and keeping them visible is the best way to have them accessible. When you come to this place in your experience of the Tules, allow yourself to take a few minutes each day just to be with the thoughts they provoke.

Look them over and think through the things you are dealing with in life. Whenever a Tule stands out, read the Compendium section on its meaning. There are strong and supporting ways to view, hold, and understand your natural thinking processes and the Tules are intended to help you see those.

The Compendium

The Compendium explains the meaning of each individual Tule. It is the central-source place for gathering those meanings as well as the correct starting ways to use Tulcidious. Until you are familiar with their meanings, refer to the Compendium's definitions and explanations for clarity about each appearance. Most of these meanings follow the dictionary definitions closely. Allow yourself to become clear about the perspective offered by the Compendium.

Throughout the individual entries in the Compendium, you will find specific suggestions of issues to examine for yourself as each Tule appears. These suggestions offer a broad generic perspective. They depict the general forms of questions to ask of yourself and they apply to the way it is suggested you use all the Tules.

The Tules consistently invite you to look within, to enter the room inside your consciousness identified by the name on each Tule, and to ask of that room what gift can be found there. As you train yourself to openly face the many challenges the questions in the Compendium will ask, you may become far more honestly familiar with your own most common ways of operating. You will see far more of what you may or may not be happy with in yourself and you will gain the opportunity of a new strength from that awareness.

A conscious commitment to allowing the benefits of the Compendium's perspective in the relationships around you can help to significantly advance the effectiveness you will know in the closest of those relationships.

Trust in your own ability to examine these things competently and allow yourself to be guided first by your own honesty. Be guided also by your most subtle feelings and allow yourself to face all the issues you see. Remember that you are alone in this process. No one is looking over your shoulder as you think and allow yourself into what a simple and sensitive honesty will offer.

The most appropriate contextual way to relate to the Tules is to see them merely as reminders. How does the appearing Tule relate to what is taking place in your life today, tomorrow, and every other day you use them?

Foremost, the Tules are about the matter of how you function in relationship with all those around you in daily life. Welcome yourself to their gifts.

Full Presence

The Full Presence Tule can be described as the home ground of wholeness and is the central access point offered by the Tules. Full Presence includes learning to continually and joyfully run in wholly new directions. It is your reality, the reality of the Self, represented here in a circle by a very simple human face, the one looking back at you from this page. See this as your face.

Full Presence is the peacefulness resulting from a personal sense of wholeness, according to your own considered yet honest definition. A person can be differently able in any way and naturally Fully Present.

Full Presence is also the invitation and challenge to take on a specifically identified thought as your own. That thought is the choice to believe in yourself as simultaneously residing in a coherent and harmonious way in all the twelve states of being that make up this group of Tules:

Blossoming, Presentation
Declaration
Discovery
Expansion
Exploration
Focusing
Meditation
Recognition
Refinement
Rest
Thanks

Tulcidious.

These twelve states of being are defined here as energetic elements that source and sustain all human creativity.

Each of these states of being is described here, in alphabetical order. They are twelve aspects of a way of thinking and being that you may know as with you all the time. The appearance of this Tule includes that specific reminder. The Full Presence Tules exist because of the right you gained at birth to Trust Yourself, the sixth of the Vibrations of the Earth.

Order is an aspect of Full Presence. This Tule also represents the natural inclusion in awareness of the whole.

The Full Presence group of Tules depicts humanity's engine for growth. The twelve states of being that make up this group collectively define a means by which we consistently accomplish creation in human life.

Working with this group of ideas is founded upon a view of us all individually as constantly growing. This view also voices the purpose of human life: for each of us to expand our Ability and Willingness to experience and express Love.

The appearance of this Tule is typically offering an acknowledgment of your state of well-being and harmony in the face of all you are dealing with in life currently. It may also be offering the suggestion that you look at the overall matters of coherence, balance, and harmony in your life. It might be suggesting that you are out of sync in some significant way.

Some suggest that a state of "self-actualization" is visible or accessible through an interpretive perspective prioritizing the centrality of this Tule. In that sense the challenge of this Tule may be to see it as holding for you the deepest opportunity for strength in reach within for good health. How do you see that suggestion as meaningful right now?

As with all the Tules, your own honesty and intuition are the guiding forces that define meaningful interpretation at any given appearance of this Tule.

> *"To be fully present includes holding all you experience whole."*

Blossoming, Presentation

To Blossom is to come into one's own, to fulfill development, like a newly discovered talent, or to make an appearance, presenting the Self for all around you to see.

The symbol in this circle is a theatrical stage shaped like an open human hand, offering the first visibility of its most recent gift, which is you.

Every form of demonstration is an aspect of Blossoming.

You are sharing yourself with everyone you meet and doing this in a way that brings newness to the task in every moment, a newness that is evident for you as well as for all those you meet.

Blossoming is an energetic home of joy.

This state also includes the seemingly passive activity of allowing unfoldment, becoming exposed, at risk, and open.

You gain from yourself all the permission you may require in order to fulfill any act of Blossoming. That grant of permission is also an aspect of Blossoming.

Blossoming is most easily recognized in the cheerful playfulness of a happy child.

Blossoming, as Presentation, includes the world of first impressions, the first impacts you create in the experience of others you have newly met.

One aspect of Blossoming is being at your work in your way, the way that works best for you.

"Can you see what being at your work in the way that works best for you actually looks like?"

When you examine this question, begin as you wake in the morning.

Declaration

Declaration is represented in this circle by any form of star.

Declaration is the act of proclaiming, announcing, or evincing a personal public notification. You are making "I am..." statements that define who you are in broad, newly honest ways. You remain open to a fiber in your being that calls for such new Declarations all the time.

You know every interaction with others as an opportunity to make new Declarations of Self. You listen to others in part through the question: "Who am I?" Declaration is how you continually build new responses.

Declaration may be accomplished by speaking, either out loud or silently within. Declaration makes an idea plain in part by use of certainty, in part by use of assertion. That expressed combination of certainty and assertion, when spoken aloud, is also how you evince commitment in the world of relationship around you.

Declarations may also be accomplished through your actions.

Declarations are the result of choice.

Declaration, whether expressed or implicit in our actions, is how we accomplish and maintain all personal relationship.

Declarations are frequently used to define personal realities and are at the essence of all human interaction.

Declaration's root and source, like that of all the Full Presence Tules, is the Sixth Vibration ~ Trust Yourself.

Loyalty may come to life as the result of Declaration and can become inherent in the elemental depths of a relationship, perhaps only, thanks to the strength of your Declarations.

All oaths are aspects of Declaration.

Declaration is also a source of certainty in relationships. If you find that hard to accept, expanding the level at which you intentionally use Declaration might help.

"Consistency is an aspect of Declaration."

Discovery

Discovery is the act or process of unfolding the otherwise unknown. Here the encircled symbol is a single arrow identifying the location of your newest surprise.

You are open always to uncovering new aspects of awareness around the nature of being itself, both for yourself and for others.

You are a fulfilled expression of the continually active presence of intentional openness to everything that elevates the level at which you know yourself and the entire world around you.

In religiously styled terms, Discovery includes the gifts of the Infinite Divine (   ).

Discovery in more specifically tangible realms is also included in the intended meaning of the concept~
What have you learned today?
What did you find today?
What did you unearth today?

Discovery is a major aspect of the process of educating yourself and of supporting yourself. Discovery includes the moment by moment experience of the result.

You are in an active state of Discovery, at some level, every moment every day. That too is a component of creativity.

Expansion

Expansion is the act or process of enlarging or giving yourself a greater scope. The symbol is a bright, unobstructed sun, here encircled. The easiest way to know this experience is to slowly take and release a large, deep breath. Even this, the merest form of engagement is an aspect of Expansion.

Expansion is elemental to the very nature of being. It is the central proactive fiber in your emotional, sensate nature by means of which you consistently open and advance yourself further and more fully toward new realms for understanding human life and new things of all kinds.

This occurs both consciously and as an openness to readily include new aspects of awareness which has become an automatic part of your daily way of life. This is another form of contextually intentional growth.

As an Expanding being, you live in a determined knowing of yourself as such. Expansion is inherent in human nature.

Expansion has a measurable starting line in conscious growth by choice. The desire for more individual comfort is not an aspect of Expansion. In this context comfort as an experience occurs as an aspect of Rest. The desire for more is an aspect of Willingness, to be found among the Lifeboat Tules.

The concept "understanding," described earlier here as a result, is an aspect of Expansion because the advancement of understanding can naturally arise by the allowing that is your choice to Expand.

Have you thought recently about where you might like to go in experience and what stands between you and that?

> *"Look within to know the self; in being, accept the self as Expansion."*

Exploration

To explore is to investigate, to search, to study, to analyze, to examine, to look into something. The symbol in this circle is an arrow-pointed, outward-going spiral.

Your every daily activity continually opens your awareness to a newly meaningful nature in everything around you.

Unimpeded Exploration consistently accomplishes the task in a way that is fully respectful of others and is accomplished in such terms independently and alone.

Exploration includes an attentive watching and listening. Both experimentation and explanation are aspects of Exploration.

Exploration includes traipsing around hearkening after something specific by choice and can be dangerous.

Thinking is an aspect of Exploration. What's the main thing on your mind today?

Focusing

To Focus is to concentrate your attention or effort on a center of activity or attraction.

The symbol in the circle here is two arrows, representing your eyes, hands, attention or awareness, identifying the location of a single particular something.

You are capable, conscious, and ready to look carefully, fully, honestly, and openly at all that comes across your path. You stop and examine the unfamiliar, the out-of-the-ordinary, and any other thing choice gives your attention to in all events and times.

Focusing is the choice to engage in a careful looking at identified components within all that you perceive and experience. This may occur as a conscious choice. Sometimes it occurs beyond that.

Focusing includes being with your own acts: acts taken, acts contemplated, and acts planned.

For most, such "being with" one's own acts is values-based. Focusing is calling your attention to those values that are individually derived. Those personal values that motivate your actions.

Focusing advances self-knowledge and awareness and thrives upon an honesty around emotions, thoughts, and human body feelings that come to life when we stop to look. Are you being honest?

"What do you see?"

Meditation

Meditation is allowing clarity to unfold as a function of freedom from distraction. The encircled symbol is three slivers of Moon locating an open whole, which is you.

Meditation includes the act or process of engaging in solitary contemplation and reflection and begins for many as a practice of emptying the mind. In such terms, some Meditation forms start with freeing oneself from all specific thought.

Other forms begin with offering a specific concept or object of attention as an aid to minimizing the distractions of thought. Some religious practitioners use the repetition of mantras to derive meditative states.

Meditation includes a choosing to be intimately engaged with the calm, free silence that lives within. One aspect of the Meditative life includes the possibility of a wide-scale peace at the center of your being, whatever your outward circumstances may be.

Meditation is an activity that affords an experience of the infinity of simplicity.

Concentration is an aspect of Meditation.

You are fully comfortable with solitary contemplation, as a result of which you can know and understanding peace in the face of any distraction. Think of Meditation as a gift of potentially divine peace.

Many agree that Meditation expands peace of mind, strengthens the body's immune system, awakens regenerative energies, slows biological aging, enlivens the nervous system, and enhances creative abilities.

Upon accepting the awareness of all such potential benefits, it remains important to remember that when you succeed fully in your experience of Meditation, the certain thing you will always find is the person sitting in your seat, the one wearing your shirt right now, still the Self as is, you.

That find is good. Meditation improves your strength.

"What does your mind contain today?"

Recognition

The symbol Recognition in this circle is the exclamation point.

Recognition is the act of admitting about yourself that you hold a particular status. You are the voice, hands, and heart of Creation itself. You know this about yourself. Others know this about you, and you and those others all know this about each other. You experience peace through these forms of knowing.

There is an aspect of Recognition that is a readiness to see yourself as a tangibly real expression of the Source or creative force known to so many as the Infinite Divine (   ).

Recognition is including as a part of your reality the admission that you are a breathing expression of the living, active creating energy of the Infinite.

Recognition identifies a great gift of being. If you accept the concept, the experience of arriving upon the awareness of Recognition may include the following progression of feeling state fibers:

Yes
Of course
surprise

Yes
resignation
anger

Yes
relief
protection

Yes
Rest.

Recognition can help you see that what matters most is every single thing you think, say, and do.

Jiddu Krishnamurti, a great sage of the 20th century, used the expression, "the process of the accumulation of experience" to refer to one part of what is called Recognition here.

Recognition includes appreciation and respect for all that you see and experience in the daily life of events and in the people around you.

The heart of all human creative ability can be found here, in Recognition.

"Understanding is also an aspect of Recognition."

Refinement

Refinement is any means to improve or perfect something. The Tules are calling your attention to the way that occurs in thought. The symbol in this circle is a moving yet contained and rounded triquetra, depicting continual active engagement inside the whole container that is you. Here the containing circle is a part of the symbol.

In human terms, Refinement is the two part process which begins with the wholly private task of honestly looking within at the way you carry yourself in your relationships and the world around you and how satisfied you are with what you see.

The second part of the Refinement process is personally and privately making the changes in your own way of operating that are called for by what you notice through that honest examination of Self.

This is choosing to change yourself by means that are carefully and personally identified. Your every moment includes a way of being that is like polishing a valuable, almost round stone. Refinement is you noticing the ways to improve and strengthen yourself, then consciously and privately putting them into place in your own life.

Refinement induces an intimate connection with one's human body feelings and always expands simplicity, consistently making life easier.

Refinement is best viewed as inwardly unidirectional. As an energetic event, see Refinement as a birthplace for components of the individual emotion experience.

For example, sadness such as that rising from the loss of a Loved one is an aspect of Refinement. When we lose a close friend, life changes substantially and we are unavoidably carried into revisions of reality as we have known it until then. Sadness is a feeling state we may think we are uncontrollably pulled into. However, we can also see it as the almost automatic adjusting to those changes in our individual reality that spirit requires. Sadness is an aspect of Refinement.

Similarly, all forms of emotional pain, including depression, are aspects of Refinement. They provide a step in awareness, sometimes the first, along a way to making changes called for by reality as we individually live it. Refinement can be how we meet the horrors we know and intentionally mold the experience to our benefit as a creative act.

Acts which might initially seem to be acts of surrender in your thinking are examples of Refinement. Where you may have been holding on to some rigidly firm positionality, and finally see a reason to do otherwise, to let go, is an aspect of Refinement. Remember that these are private occurrences in thought. To release, to let go and give where you have (long) not is Refinement.

The reparative activity that frees you from worry is also an aspect of Refinement. If you feel extremely fragmented or scattered in facing some feature of your daily life, what it means is that you are in the perfectly natural process of personal change, an aspect of Refinement.

Recognizing initially confronting experiences as aspects of Refinement can make it easier for you to carry yourself to a place of calm about any such emotional matters. Your ability to simply have the name for what's taking place is the start of hefting and exercising authority over it all more competently.

You can say to yourself, *"Ah, I'm not being overwhelmed by an immensity of problems I can't handle. Instead, I'm in the midst of a major change and changing myself as I see necessary along the way to meet the challenge the most fully well."* That's Refinement. That's you.

Refinement is a common experience we all live with daily. Merely understanding the nature of what you are facing and the fact that this kind of personal examination is a typical aspect of life can help you more frequently carry yourself to a place of peace and make it possible to come at any moment of necessary change with new equanimity. In this way, Refinement applies to all the issues you face in daily life, more than just those that make up who you are.

The benefit of knowing and using this name for the component of the thinking process that is pointed to by the distinction is perhaps the central core component of our common potential for intelligent and mature consciousness because it is by means of the reality of the act of self-driven, intentional choice that we recognize our authority over the daily life experience of our circumstances, wherever we stand in those. Refinement is Creation.

Refinement may be seen like a catcher's mitt. Every fearful experience or thought is purposefully serving grounds for the question, "what opportunity lies here?" In this situation to look at one's own inadequacies or inability to see resides not as the stuff of a meaningful or necessary assessment of self. Instead and in fact, to look in this way presents the opportunity to feed the awareness of a storehouse in consciousness of beneficial experience we stand upon as creators, while knowing the self as a discoverer, calmly, slowly pausing to examine your thinking or experiential reality, as you open your own doors to vision.

This advances the importance of the release from self-judgment, unspoken in the description of the Contrast Tule, and of seeing the energies that lead to self-judgment first as passing, unimportant thoughts, then as including some stuff of being you now see to hold differently, as the stuff of Refinement.

Specifically, this Tule is also inviting you to notice prominently that those emotional, vibrational, and spiritual energies you have used until now to derive and place judgments against yourself are real, and more importantly, misdirected and misused when in that manner. This Tule is the reminder that those energies are better intended and more wisely, perhaps even more naturally, used instead to feed the daily progress of re-examination, and so to create by making new choice frames for yourself as the reaching act of growth. To do so is Love.

Completion is an aspect of Refinement.

Do you see other emotional processes you experience that you would call aspects of Refinement?

> "Mere observation is strength.
> To commit is to exist."

Rest

Alone in your own favorite or most comfortable space.

Rest is a bodily state of peace of mind or spirit. The symbol in this circle is a sleeping face.

You are expanding your readiness through relaxation at every moment, quietly and consistently advancing your sense of preparedness for all of life's frustrating confrontations.

This state includes frequent gentle calming experiences of all kinds, accomplished by choice.

Large deep breaths, which are the conscious choice to stop and breathe with awareness, bring on a state of ease, which is Rest. Some say every exhale is an aspect of Rest. Any giving attention to your breath is Rest.

Giving blood is an aspect of Rest. Any simple joy can be an aspect of Rest. Relax.

Taking a walk may be restful for you. Being alone, engaged in any form of non-stressful activity, might be Rest for you. Sleep is Rest for most. Fully engaged in some favorite activity, with the music you most like playing, might be Rest for some.

"Relaxation facilitates insight."

Thanks

Thanks includes kindly or grateful thoughts. The symbol in this circle is one, using two hands to Thank another.

Thanks can include an aspect of praise for that which you revere as Divine (   ). All expressions of gratitude are aspects of Thanks.

Whenever we pay anyone for anything, one of the things we are doing is expressing Thanks.

You live in appreciation. You share, experience, and think through appreciation in all that you do. This is true both as a part of your Nature and to the extent that you accept the idea as a component of your conscious awareness.

Thanks can have many giving forms, including statements of congratulation, money, smiles, laughter, food, shelter, kind words spoken or written, a look in the eye, a touch of the hand, a hug, pleasure, relief, and many more.

Sharing Thanks can also be a source of joy.

Tulcidious

The word and Tule Tulcidious supply a mechanism for connecting with an identifiable conception generally described as follows~

It is possible to know the reality of human awareness where 'awareness' can be called an aspect of consciousness (I am aware that I think, therefore I am aware of the reality of thinking). Thinking is a component of consciousness. Looking at the reality of your ability to think about something identifies what is called an awareness of that something (I can think about this green apple; therefore, I have an awareness of it). One component of the reality awareness gives us may be the single common connection most nearly known to all humanity, the idea of caring for another. Caring.

Now so visibly isolated in all the universe of our existence, it can be said that our Earth has "shrunken" to a size we may understand as never before. Among all so many other things, we notice our differences and our feelings about those differences as we also examine the features of what we know to be possible around our individual means to isolate ourselves. Caring is the choice that supplies the experience of acceptance, for both yourself and others, which can lead to comfort and peace. Caring in this manner serves as a bridge. Similarly, education, risk, and vulnerability are bridges.

A component of consciousness as common as mere caring may be thought of as identifying the existence of an agenda, though saying so immediately raises the question, to what end? The only possible whole response to that question is, "every end that goes by that name." More important than these nuances of definition is grasping responsible hold of the reality we have, irrespective of what we'd most like.

Caring, a component of Love, has an agenda; that agenda is known to human consciousness. The weight of that consciousness includes some part of all the human awareness of every person who has ever lived and everything they each lived to achieve and to hope for. A summation of the whole of this view named *Tulcidious* can then be summarized by saying that Tulcidious is living in the accomplished awareness of the wholly pervasive presence of Love in all times and places.

Tulcidious is the name the author has given to his stated interpretation of caring, as we may arguably be seen to have it collectively, approximately at the time of the turn of the twenty-first century. The word itself is derived from the name of Tulsidas, a Hindu poet who is believed to have lived between 1497, or 1532, or 1543 and 1623 (all CE). How you may alone and personally see the precision of the author's conclusions identified here is the gift of who you are.

To use the word, Tulcidious, is to make the claim that the agenda of caring is permanently in place in the affairs of all humanity, everywhere on and connected to the Earth that human consciousness has carried itself throughout all time until now. If humanity holds authority within its own affairs, we may see, in part through the choice to accept ideas of this kind, that a firm, consistent, identifiable, and clear direction for guiding human action may be found in such terms and that acceptance of that direction can have a beneficial impact upon the achievement of humanity's success in our collective role as stewards of the planet and its place in service to human consciousness.

To use the word, Tulcidious, is to walk with a clarity you may be said to already possess in some greater or lesser degree. This is clarity in the form of an absolute, certain knowing that the full strength of human consciousness is connected permanently to the ultimate purposes of the universe, and that all is well in the accomplishment of those purposes, at that massively broad level, in your individual life, and at every place and level in between. Expanding your acceptance of this as an awareness can be a source of great peace.

The symbol in this circle is a single line that depicts visually a common form of the style in progression of events that advance the reality of Tulcidious in life.

See it as a bridge that picks you up gently, carries you to a great height of vision, then rather suddenly to the lowest depths, and finally very gradually allowing you out of that, leaves you again gently in a place just slightly more specifically advanced than when and where you began. Expanding moments in the conscious awareness of Tulcidious can be like that, including the greatest of highs, followed by shockingly difficult lows all of which, after complete exhaustion, can leave you in a state of gentle though great surprise, and make knowing that ultimate change very subtle, yet deeply transformative.

Advancing your awareness of the pervasive presence of Love in your life and in all human affairs is also more than a one-time experience. The Tule, Tulcidious, like all the other Full Presence Tules, identifies a state of your being, an inherent feature of your very humanness. This is true for every human.

The Tules rise from a view of reality that recognizes and respects Love as the Creative Force that carried all existence as humans can know it, all humans and all life, into being. It would serve you to glance now at your hands or into a mirror and take a moment to examine your Willingness to believe that those hands, your hands, are the hands of Love, that your face and your consciousness are a face and consciousness breathed into life by Love. You may have judgments of doubt about yourself in this regard yet those are merely measures of the level of your own acceptance.

Tulcidious is an enlarged connection to all existence that expands in part by conscious choice.

Acknowledging the concept here named Tulcidious as a component or inherent "state" of your being, and as a connection to the accepted perfection of all human reality and all larger reality, will relieve you of fear more fully and successfully than any other act or choice you may ever know. You are certainly free to name or conceive of the experience for yourself in such terms or in any other way you like. The peculiar word, "Tulcidious" is the name the author constructed specifically as a means for acknowledging your freedom in this regard.

Tulcidious is hallmarked by the ability to recognize that every other person you meet, however they may each choose to express themselves in relation to you, is expressing Love in the best way that he or she knows how, given all of that person's life, experience, and ability. Just as paying for something always includes a component of Thanks, Tulcidious reminds you that whatever else is taking place, whatever else that other person is doing, he or she, consciously or otherwise, is in part making a best effort at caring. When we are distressed by the acts of others, to live Tulcidious is to share an ever-larger, responsible compassion.

Tulcidious is then a multi-sensual awareness of that caring fiber in every human heart, no matter what troubles may be given life by any other being, thing, or experience. It is a "larger knowing" that transcends all contextual perceptions of conflict.

Tulcidious is the fiber in your awareness that allows you the kind, reparative methodological act of viewing any viciousness, and everything like it, as an aspect of either fear or confusion, or both. Remember here though, and regarding everything you read in this book, that neither compassion nor any form of caring license the bad faith that would farm to produce their requirement or encouragement.

Tulcidious is an invitation to consider the idea that you are inherently capable of knowing an intentional peacefulness as a defined aspect of your Nature, even perhaps that such access to peacefulness is the central core of being that defines every human, while the advancement of common consciousness accomplishes carrying more to the same place.

Anger, fear, upset, conflict, and war are all aspects of Tulcidious because our ability to release these concepts from our actions and lives may be accomplished by first acknowledging the existence of an identified reality, which is Love. Remember that we are all striving toward a common goal which is ultimately a kaleidoscopic mutuality, resident in successful relationship. Today, amid this, war isn't so much wrong as it is pointless, an aimless, inexcusable, habitual set of repetitive actions in reactivity, born in an ancient time bound to struggles for mere survival, all of which humanity's better angels have surmounted today.

Can you see it as possible for you to think that the other who is hurting you, even if in a way that you experience as intentional and malicious, is doing the best at human decency that he or she knows how (of course primarily motivated by fear) in the face of all that is his or her life? The fear that sources destructive acts today most frequently rises from harmed early life training around the infinities of possibility and environments of unfairness, hardship, or indifference. The resultant fear is an understandable and predictable ignorance of the full nature of relationship. The ability to see and accept these ideas includes a sparking to life of both compassion and commitment.

Can you see the idea that if our world exists for the purpose of expanding the genuine daily life experience of the affirmation of life through kindness and caring for us all, then an "enlightened" view of confrontations with hurt sees them as most accurately viewed as opportunities, something like grist for a mill that produces Love, the elemental product of all human purpose? The extremely difficult act of "turning the other cheek" when someone does us harm, if we can know we do so with a consciously identified intentional purpose, has a home in this view.

Can you allow yourself to see unavoidable conflict as food for Love? Can you see the idea that if you are connected to some large-scale conflict like a war, your first role is to always ask, in whatever way your circumstances make possible, "why war or any form of violence at all?" Given the state of human civilization now, the same challenge applies to every smaller event of conflict in your life, far more than merely the large-scale confrontations of nations and ideologies.

Even if you miss addressing this challenge, or see yourself as wholly unable to face it, merely recognizing the question is an aspect of Tulcidious and fulfills you more, advancing the pervasive presence of Love in human awareness and experience by whatever small measure your acknowledgment accomplishes. The central purpose of human existence is advanced and fulfilled more by every such acknowledgment, even if occurring only in thought. That is consciousness.

Destructive energies will always need to be stopped, but a destructive energy, unleashed by another, causes movement which can and must be dealt with, the worst effects of which may be possible to allay apart from their initiator. Separately and at the receiving end, the shift in your consciousness to mere awareness of our caring nature as humans can help the one who pulled the trigger to understand that doing so is pointless because your choice for shift eviscerates the fear in you that might otherwise found the desire for revenge.

Consequences have long been a pervasive motivator of our actions. Advancing your personal sense of Tulcidious makes it possible to see a more genuine motivational reality, that unleashing destructive energies aimed at other humans is contrary to human nature. Those who continue to insist that war and any other models of problem-solving based in violence are appropriate to resolving human dilemmas, are best rightly viewed now like living dinosaurs~ ultimately extinct but undeniably large, real, and exceedingly dangerous. Our willingness to respect these conclusions advances the authority of our intelligence over the visceral and reactive manner that rose with humanity from the depths of our evolutionary history.

Humans are all in the same predicament of frailty. This inescapable reality requires of all responsible consciousness the admission that to do harm to any other is to do harm to oneself, even if only in thought.

More importantly, our common purposes deserve our energy, vitality, and attention more than our sometimes tendencies to denigrate each other for one or another reasons, always rising from some further fear.

Can it then be accurate to say that the crime is to be denigrated, rather than your brother, the one you would call a criminal? If you can share the strength to care for him as you do for yourself, you might come to call him by the name, Tulcidious, or by your own name, as a means for personally accepting that ultimately collective human mutuality. You might also think to wonder what may have motivated him to his criminal act and what change apart from him might free him from that motivation in times to come.

Humanity will not fail itself because it has not committed itself to advancing to the real end of violence. If humanity fails it will be because of a denial of even the possibility that its understandable history of commitment to violence could come to a naturally evocative and fulfilling end because our intelligence and ability were finally stronger. We have more important things to spend our resources and attention upon.

How we may sometimes operate in response to such challenges as these can be said until now to have most frequently resided in a different realm, described next by the Lifeboat Tules.

"Tulcidious is a pathway to common ground."

The Lifeboat

"Give a name to your choice, then ask what meaning it has in your life."

Each of the nine Lifeboat Tules may be thought of as a multi-sided coin, even though only a single concept is specifically identified by each. In the simplest example, honesty is an aspect of Integrity (Integrity is the second Tule in the group). The phrase, "is an aspect of" is specifically intended to suggest that Integrity has many "aspects" helping to define the idea, honesty being merely one of them. When the Integrity Tule appears for you, it might be an acknowledgment of (a commendation for) your honesty or it might be serving to call your attention to some lack of honesty on your part, or even on the part of others you may be dealing with. You are the judge of all such matters.

The nine Lifeboat Tules, in the order presented here, are:

> Presence for the Self
> Integrity
> Trust
> Responsibility
> Contrast
> Time
> Willingness
> Ability
> Freedom.

Each of these nine Lifeboat Tules has nine sides.

Your personal honesty with yourself is the foundation on which all the Tules rest. You will succeed at using them the most effectively if you focus your attention on how they speak to or for yourself rather than the others around you.

The Lifeboat is a symbolic compilation of tools humans have used for survival throughout our long history and in the process of civilizing ourselves. Their separation from the Full Presence Tules is, at the first, a way of distinguishing between the concept of survival skills and the broader realm of creativity depicted by the other group. The distinction is in part intended to show you merely one way of understanding the nature of processes you may sense in your thinking, shared with a view to making your daily life easier by helping you separate fibers of thought in a simple, tangible, clear and understandable way.

Though they may identify the manner of our most common confrontations and struggles, there is no intent here to denigrate the concept of survival skills. They are essential basics of understanding and they hallmark major features of the successful human way. The way to use the Lifeboat Tules most constructively is to look for the opportunities of Expansion that the awareness they supply will offer.

The first is again the face of the Self. Full Presence, although here the concept is introduced with a slightly different name, which unfolds another aspect of meaning.

> *"The honest welcome of truth defines a healthy standard in an emergency world."*

Presence for the Self

In the movie, *Titanic*, when the last of the ship's stern finally went under, the film's hero, Jack Dawson, was pulled apart from his Love and far under water by the suction caused by the sinking ship. He was determined to make certain that Rose survived. In order to save her, though, he had to first save himself from drowning. In the extreme, Presence for the Self is the choice to save yourself, as he did, in all such moments.

Being present for others necessitates being Present for the Self first. The symbol in this nonagon is again the face that represents the Self. This Tule is nine-sided, as are all the Lifeboat Tules.

Presence for the Self is an intimately connected fiber of Full Presence. As such it is rightly seen as the leading head of a tangent that proceeds out from the elemental central point of human existence and reality that is your individual sense of Full Presence. Maybe you can see the rest of the Lifeboat group of Tules as the tail of that tangent, like the tail following a comet. Imagining that tangent to be one of many may also help you to gain a perspective on the larger and more expansive features of universal reality.

In these terms, Presence for the Self is the first imperative for us all. As an imperative, it is wholly justified in all circumstances, not merely those in which our lives are threatened.

Remember though that greed, indifference~ calculated or otherwise, selfishness, and their more subtle forms are not aspects of Presence for the Self. Instead, they are predictable expressions of fear occurring in relationship and, as such, aspects of Integrity, the starting place within the Lifeboat of all relationship.

Presence for the Self includes respect for yourself. The concept of mere noticing is an aspect of Presence for the Self.

Balance, in whatever form that idea has meaning for you, is an aspect of Presence for the Self. Presence for the Self is not accomplished by intentionally doing harm to others. We fail when operating by means of conscious indifference toward the expense of others.

Presence for the Self includes a conscious awareness around the elements of your individual diet. That is, everything you consume, both in terms of the food, drink, and chemical elements you send in through your mouth, nose, and skin, as well as the experiences you consume.

If, for example, you notice that the amount of time you spend driving a car or watching television depicts an avoidance of your intentional purposes rather than serving them, then you are missing the point, leaving yourself out, not being Present for the Self.

A chance selection of this Tule might be a commendation, or it might be a reminder to re-examine what you think is possible around the matter of how well you care for yourself. We cannot be available to serve or merely even be effectively present for others in any impactfully accomplishing way without caring for ourselves first, in all matters, times and events. This is a rule without exceptions. It may be that component in the heart of consciousness most fully affording our survival. The choice both to be and to continue to be.

All affirmations of individuality fail when affirming unbridled indifference toward others or any license to do harm.

Presence for the Self is a voice for happiness. Use it to ask yourself this question: Do you have a happy home? If you have questions about that, look at what you think is possible. One of the boundaries of reality for most is the limits defined by what we believe to be possible. Being engaged in such looking is an aspect of Presence for the Self.

Presence for the Self supplies the opportunity to set forth your enthusiasm around where and how it is that we become the most highly well connected with and among ourselves and each other.

Presence for the Self includes welcoming. When given into life as any kind of welcoming to one or more others, Presence for the Self is an honoring of the self. This is an act of Loving Yourself that supplies a "precision of existence moment" experience which is a form of requiring of the self also much like a birth. This is the vibrational requiring that gives Integrity into existence, a kind of leap of being seen in these terms as the Grand Leap. Here is the heart of the reality, I am.

As you allow yourself the awareness in understanding that Presence for the Self is an unlimited right granted to each of us by Nature, you can come to just as naturally see the same right in every other. That bit of common Nature is a component of the kaleidoscopic and joyous mutuality intended by the Divine ( ) for the benefit of all humanity. It is a gift of graciousness fully served to forward our arrival upon the day intended to affirm our successful accomplishment in thriving relationship with a wholly symbiotic world.

> *"Let pass the very thought of wanting to bother with not knowing yourself."*

Integrity

Violence is anathema to truth. The ship's down. After you save yourself, do your best to help save anyone else.

This, at the very least, is kindliness, one aspect of Integrity. The symbol in this nonagon is a series of five individual lines depicting soundness as a whole.

Integrity is formally defined as a firm adherence to a code of values or a set of standards; also as an unimpaired condition of soundness and as the quality or state of being complete or undivided.

For purposes of the Tules, Integrity is the skill identified by your conscious choice to achieve a complete and unimpaired condition of soundness inclusive of the character features described here and accomplished through firm adherence to a code of values or a set of standards not based in the doing of harm, where soundness includes freedom from injury, disease, flaw, defect, or decay.

Integrity is the natural state of beneficial relationship. This is the meaningful detail.

Integrity includes honesty, sincerity, fidelity, frankness, honor, authenticity, loyalty, respect, trustworthiness, and fairness. Integrity also includes candor, which is honest or sincere expression free from bias, prejudice, and malice.

Although many of these features of Integrity can be listed and introduced with just one word, none of them are insignificant matters. Do you understand the meaning of each of these concepts? Every appearance of this Tule requires that you advance with Ability and Willingness your experience of the genuine nature of Integrity in your life and the manner of how you honestly give expression to that in relationship with everyone around you.

When this Tule appears, be honest with yourself in facing issues you know are present and examine them more carefully than you might normally. Only some of the prominent features concerning Integrity are specifically addressed here and only by way of example. It is entirely appropriate to consider as well, at a full greater length, any of these listed concepts (or others you know to be features of Integrity for you) that attract your attention, because they all so significantly impact the relationships in our lives.

The relationships in your life are the final proving ground for truth.

As just one example, do you see yourself as operating fairly in your daily life? The word, "fairly," as used in the prior sentence, is a reference to the idea of *Fairness* which is characterized particularly by freedom from fraud, injustice, prejudice, and undue favoritism, even toward oneself. Looked at directly, the small four-letter word, "fair," identifies a high yet appropriate standard for our Integrity. In all realms of competition, fairness includes not utilizing practices that would be condemned by law as violating the public interest.

Respecting that definition, do you utilize fair practices in your daily life at work? Does your employer?

Is it also possible that your sense of Integrity would be easier to maintain if you found it meaningful to operate from a ground of being based entirely <u>beyond</u> competition?

Consider alternatively a ground of being based in collaboration. How does your view shift when you look for collaborative options? Does the idea of collaboration offer any meaningful or beneficial sense of purpose for you? Can you imagine that a collaborative way of being might improve your sense of personal satisfaction in the relationships around you? Can it be that widening your experience of Integrity in fairness may also rise from acknowledging and giving expression to a sense of connection in collaboration rather than the isolating alternative of competition, the latter in a transformed world respectful of Spirit being fully visible as a form of violence?

Integrity also includes "virtue," which is defined in part as "conformity to a standard of right" such as a sense of ethics. This is your personal connection with the standards for thought, speaking, and action that you may have chosen to respect, along with your relationship among those other persons, groups, animals, or things that are the beneficiaries of your virtue.

Your conscious choice of standards identifies the primary elemental essence of who you are. That choice is the founding ground in life for the possibility of the golden rule of relationship that calls us all to treat others as we ourselves wish to be treated.

The perspective offered by the Tules includes the emphatic reminder that this is choice, calling for your fullest genuineness, rather than something pre-ordained or imposed upon you from outside. To live at choice in this realm is to rise for the experience of others in your fullest nature as a free creator of good, fully affirmed by the Divine ( ). When you are aware of this choice, it can provide you great strength. When you live your daily life as these forms of choices you feed the truth of Love. Can it be true that there is nothing more the Divine ( ) can wish for you?

While environment, culture, religions, philosophies and the daily challenges of life itself may press you hard in one direction or another, you are here to give full expression to the gift of free choice that defines you, both in relationship and in how you see yourself.

The "Eightfold Path" of Buddhism is one example of a known set of standards around which you can test your personal sense of those choices you consider most meaningful. The appearance of this Tule includes the invitation to do that. Test your sense of Integrity as defined by those standards you know most precisely define you. There are many other such examples. How many do you know?

If the Tule's reminder to look in that way seems complex or difficult for you, the starting place remains the question, are you being fully honest with yourself and in communication with all those around you?

Deceit, greed, selfishness, and turpitude, all of which are offensive to Integrity, are in consequence aspects of it, in part because they all regard the matter of how you relate to others, and the mere reality of such acts of bad faith will impair your standing in Integrity. Every appearance of the Integrity Tule is calling into question every act you know is of bad faith or questionable sincerity. Are you being honest and fair with those around you?

By this means, the Integrity Tule, like all the others, is specifically intended to carry your attention to concepts that could seem to be expressions of its opposites or alternatives. Are you operating in a manner that does harm to another? Doing any form of harm to anyone else impairs the wholeness in your Integrity. Whenever you know this to be true, the question of Integrity offers the requirement of your personal and honest evaluation. To view the matter any other way is to deny another individual the level of humanity that you would grant yourself while also adding limitation to your openness and humanness.

The Integrity Tule is also intended in part to call your attention to the reality that matters such as war and capital punishment are aspects of relationship, and hence aspects of Integrity. In today's immensely complex world, we each reach unique personal conclusions in all matters of Integrity. It is unrealistic to suggest or believe that the values we individually respect will apply with the same outcomes to all other people and circumstances. The only meaningful standard may perhaps be defined by the level of dishonor in the degree to which you believe you have a right to consciously act in a manner that produces harm or imposes suffering on others. Today it is myopic, and perhaps dishonest, even to think that violence and the calculated doing of harm in either your actions or speaking can be normative or justifiable in any way.

Remember that the Tules are not intended to define rules, but rather to reaffirm your awareness of the choices we all face, and to call your own attention to how you resolve them. It may not be possible to define a universally consistent "right path" other than one respecting the reality that we are all unique and equally frail individuals deserving of freedom from outside oppression and entitled to each other's compassion and respect.

The Tules supply permission to expand the level at which you respect yourself. This means they are calling you to look within more fully and honestly than you ever have before at the reality of your own charge in life. They are also intended to cause you to look at issues you may never have looked directly at before, from an awareness that you are individually and exclusively the source of all your experience.

When the Integrity Tule appears, examine fully the way you relate to others. All your firm "positions" in relationship are aspects of Integrity. Where you recognize your own "positionality," challenge the level of rigidity that identifies and examine whether you have formed your views for yourself. If you have not, ask yourself why. Look the most carefully at the degree to which fear, particularly of loss, may be ruling or defining your views, and perhaps even the manner of your very being.

The first time the Integrity Tule appears for you, or now, use it as an invitation to examine anew all aspects of your relational ways. Individual, familial, communal, national, human, spiritual, and metaphysical. Look at all the places you have wanted to go in relationship throughout your life until today. Look with particular care at, and question, the part that a violent state of mind may play in your thinking. Look at how you stand in your relationships. Look at what you believe to be possible in all the relationships of which you are a part. Look at the permission you grant to yourself and how this is limited by what you consider possible. Look at the degree to which your Integrity impacts all these things.

Every appearance of the Integrity Tule is an invitation into all these matters. You will experience the Tules far more successfully and with much greater strength if you will allow yourself the in-depth examination with that first appearance, or this.

Do the best you can, and be honest with yourself, knowing that you are well accompanied. When you reach the other side you will know how to enjoy laughing at yourself.

> *"Relationship is everything."*

Trust

Trust is a forward-looking, confident anticipation rising from a feeling of security and inspiring reliance upon the character, ability, strength, or truth of some other person or thing.

The symbol in this nonagon is one leaning on another.

This Tule concerns your Trust of others, one of the primary means by which we extract ourselves from the weight of individual solitude around matters of significant concern. Trust is the foundation of leadership and a primary component of constructive relationship.

When this Tule appears examine whether you can believe that opening yourself to newly Trusting another might advance your sense of strength around one or more of the concerns you are carrying. At a personal level, the communication essential to constructively beneficial Trust advances friendship, partnership, intimacy, and emotional maturity generally. Constructing the ability to speak, even for slightest measures of help, is an aspect of Trust, and regularly reduces the impacts of confusion.

Sharing Trust also builds Trust (a mutuality, strengthening of everyone it touches). Expanding Trust advances the legitimacy of civilized society and can work especially well when you are confused or lost at sea and wonder why.

When you are moved or invited by the Tule to consider placing new Trust in another, remember that Trust rises from an inspiring feeling. This means that the advancement of your Trust does not rightly occur merely because you have heard that Trust is a good idea or because you read somewhere that Trust makes life easier. A hoped-for possibility of more ease is not a reason to expand your Trust. Instead, in this context the Expansion of ease is a result that can rise from a legitimately founded choice on your part. Respecting the definition of Trust stated above, this means a choice founded in your feelings, inspired by the "character, ability, strength, or truth of some other person or thing."

When this Tule appears and the opportunity to offer new Trust becomes apparent, listen to the voice of the confidence and security that your intuition may be sensing, rather than that of the fear you already know. It is inspired confidence, rather than hope for a reduction in pain or fear, that comports with the true nature of Trust.

Sharing Trust is important because it is both forward looking and brave, consistently involving a risk on your part that a result you may anticipate will not be fulfilled. Granting your Trust to another can be particularly risky also because it is easy to fall from a sought-after, preferred, or anticipated result to the thought that your grant of Trust permits some right to an expectation on your part, which is a form of requirement no right to which comes to life merely because you Trust someone. Mere Trust cannot guarantee a result or give you the right to require a guaranteed result. This points to one of the further realities around Trust, that you cannot precisely know in advance the exact features of the results your Trust may found.

Trust finds birth in this field of uncertainty where the risk of non-fulfillment is fully exposed. When you notice a feeling state that weakens your sense of risk, the reason may be genuine grounds for sharing your Trust.

Even if you fully understand and recognize these distinctions (and importantly if you do not), you might also feel a desire to take the risk of advancing your Trust in another without knowing this precisely identified feeling state. When you are looking to share Trust but are not moved to do so by any strong feeling of inspired ability to rely upon another, your choice will accurately identify the level of risk you are open to.

Speaking aloud with that other to describe your thoughts or feelings in such a moment can always reduce the level of that risk and is the choice for an act of creative bravery which will help you derive clarity very likely not otherwise possible. Such an act opens a valuable awareness of who you are to both that other and yourself, also expanding opportunity, possibility, and overall health, always limiting the kind of confusion that so easily rises from non-communication.

It is also true that your intuition and bodily feeling states can deliver a message so subtle, and rising from a naturalness so simple, that you may not even notice some new placement of Trust you have already accomplished. Have you begun to newly Trust someone without noticing? Have you newly noticed some long-held sense of Trust? If so, this Tule may only be aiding you in identifying a new foundation or fiber of satisfaction in your life. Perhaps new grounds for both Trust and Thanks. When this is so, allow yourself to acknowledge the joy.

I.
Removing Trust

The Trust Tule also invites the question whether some Trust you have already placed in another is rightly so placed. When noticing yourself in conscious doubt as to the rectitude of an existing placement of Trust in another person, call yourself first always to approach that person in conversation before retreating from the tangible aspects of the investment of Trust.

Where you are honestly certain that your common communication is clear and lacking any misunderstanding, such an act hallmarks the deepest respect where possible as certain not to cause harm. Communicating before withdrawing your Trust identifies commitment and respect in your view of relationship.

Today, as you will see while reading about the Tule, Responsibility, the appearance of this Tule is calling you to a careful personal examination that respects the prior imperative of Presence for the Self and all the challenges of Integrity, before removing your Trust without communicating openly with the other person, as fully as that is honestly possible.

The strength of confidence called for by this is a component of the gift you and your Trusted are together and identifies an advanced and complex investment of emotional energy. When confronted, or earlier in anticipation of that, being quick to mapping some better, safer, secretive, or generally one-sided way out proves insincere as weak, and may be motivated merely by a sense of solitude in fear of loss, or other forces encircling the basis of your Trust that have yet to be fully examined. Look.

While listening for the larger response in compassion here, on the appearance of this Tule mind stuff of these kinds can also be pointing to needless aggression as a motive energy in you. Where this is visible, we are reminded to question and challenge the drive vibration of attack in ourselves. This work exists in part to gather attention for the existence of such (attached-to-attack manner) drive vibrations. All vibrations of aggression are suspect, and it is brave to guard against them like dangerous ancient monsters. On the noticing, consider how to release all sense of 'drive by aggression' motivation from your life and attention, willingly and readily.

To question or disarm the motivating validity of a thought of attack is to release feelings of fear. Well-being thrives in an atmosphere released of the weight of non-communication motivated by or carrying burdens of aggression. The observation of an alternative of openness, as pointed to by this and many of the Tules, as well as numerous famous written works, may help you see patterns derived from your past experiences that no longer serve your character.

This view of Trust also identifies the importance of looking at what you use Trust to accomplish, and whether you do that honestly, a subtlety honorably bound to your experience of the Integrity Tule.

Community rises from Trust. Remember that Trust, like all acts of Love, is a moment by moment outward moving cast of energy that most frequently exists without any speaking at all. Your choices around Trust paint your view of relationship.

In using this and all the Tules, look for the opportunities of new grounding in honesty offered for your life. Those opportunities are invitations to such honesty and to all the questions they inspire for you, today and every other day the Tule appears.

> *"Trust is the key to coherence."*

Responsibility

Responsibility helps to provide context for our lives, most notably when we are dealing with a calamity such as a sinking ship or any other eventuality presenting the moment by moment wholly unknown. This nonagon's symbol is the hands of a clock displaying the time 9 AM.

A Responsibility is an obligation in the nature of a burden which one chooses willingly to bind oneself to or accept. Such an obligation is commonly in the form of an agreement to take certain action which may or may not be specifically defined. As an example, a child's first pet would naturally come with the Responsibility for its care, although the child might not initially recognize that such Responsibility could include an array of specific activities it would become required of her to perform.

Aspects of Responsibility~ Authority

One component of Responsibility is the authority to do the required in order to accomplish our tasks successfully. The young child's Responsibility for the care of her new puppy will then naturally include the right to tell her father when the supply of puppy food is running low. It is an important part of parenthood (and teaching Responsibility) to make certain that the child in such a situation is aware of this right. When we succeed at making her aware of that, then this most simple example effectively depicts the authority of managerial supervision. The empowered child is "in charge of" supervising the supply of dog food, an aspect of her Responsibility for the animal's care. If you have young children, what do you do to help them come to understand the first Responsibilities you would have them know?

Aspects of Responsibility~ Obligations

When the Responsibility Tule appears, use it first as an opportunity to look at the level at which you are succeeding with your own specifically obligated performances. Are you completely fulfilling all of what you know to be your existing Responsibilities? If you have any uncertainty in this area, the Tule is suggesting that you look very carefully to admit to yourself what you know to be the truth about that.

Because they are obligations that arise by agreement, Responsibilities are relational, involving other people. It is an irresponsible pitfall to hold undescribed expectations of other people, yet it is an important part of examining one's own Responsibilities to look at what expectations others may hold of you. The expectations of others may arise as a function of the obligations you have consciously accepted as well as the stated forms of relationship you have chosen.

Paradoxically, and right or wrong, expectations concerning your obligations of action can also arise in the mind of another and begin as undescribed or unstated (not mentioned to you).

Although the unstated expectation of one does not inherently define the Responsibility of another, some Responsibilities can arise from culturally implied expectations. Other seemingly unstated Responsibilities may be imposed by law.

Responsibilities founded in culturally implied expectations are commonly seen by those others who would impose them (again rightly or wrongly) as naturally occurring and as real and firm as any fully described obligation. This reference to cultural implications acknowledges the frequently defining quality of family ties, which for many also include the influences of religious tradition. As you look at what's so for you in these areas, be both honest with and true to yourself. Culture and its attendant influences can press the most heavily into your reality when the questions at hand regard the defining of your Responsibilities, what another may believe them to be, or think or feel about how they are rightly derived or fulfilled.

Your mere awareness of this makes it important to face all your connections and relationships in a way that is honest and fully communicative, rather than minimal and avoiding. Doing so is a personal choice, yet the enthusiastic, honest communication being suggested can also immensely increase your strength, even your sense of life as joy. Be reminded again that you are the final judge of how these issues play out in your life.

You might choose one or more specific acts or courses of conduct because of the influence of some culturally oriented concept or out of a respect for an identifiable "tradition," but if you do, be certain that the choice rises from a personal conclusion about who you are rather than who someone else may wish you to be. You fail your personal identity if your choices concerning the world around you rise from anywhere other than what you know and believe of yourself from within.

The perspective from which the Tules arise includes an intent to identify a stated pathway for participation in life that would challenge you to bring yourself to the table of Responsibility with all the enthusiasm you can see to use. Have you made yourself fully aware of the obligations specifically or impliedly imposed upon you by the full array of your relationships? Have you faced your own feelings regarding the attitudes displayed by the others who may readily be willing to impose obligations upon you? At the least, these are questions about how openly you communicate. Building yourself in this area is teaching yourself with truth. Allow yourself to be ruled by who you know you are.

It can also occur that another will hold un-described expectations of you that are neither reasonable nor possible to anticipate. When this occurs, it is most likely the result of that other person's fear. Remember that your choice or determination to act responsibly does not guarantee that others will do the same or even know how. How you relate to that situation is another potential entry point for both compassion and the challenge to Expand your conscious ability at honest communication, where honesty is being true to yourself and your own word.

In the realm of priorities, remember that among the Lifeboat Tules the first, Presence for the Self, does come first. All else yields to the imperative of your personal preservation. Unless of course the time has come to give or offer your life for something you view as having a larger or more meaningful purpose than your life in the body in which you now reside. If that is true, you would rightly be described as brave.

Responsibility defines the imperative of diplomacy.

Throughout humanity's history very many have given or risked their lives to support communal, national or religious causes they believed in, frequently considering the doing so a Responsibility. Sacrificing our lives or placing them at risk by choice in this way, however, when not in a situation of emergency, *without a careful personal examination that respects the prior imperative of Presence for the Self and all the challenges of Integrity*, is no longer necessary and more importantly, no longer appropriate to any legitimate human purpose. Not for anyone. That *"careful personal examination that respects the prior imperative of Presence for the Self and all the challenges of Integrity,"* is the heart of Responsibility simply because, by its very nature, no Responsibility arises other than by conscious choice.

No Responsibility can be imposed upon you from outside yourself, other than by duress, which is being forced to do something against your own will. Anyone who tells you otherwise is working to deceive you, and very likely deceived themselves.

All genuine Responsibilities arise as the result of individual conscious choice. "Conscious" here means with knowledge, intent, and purpose. If you are being called upon by someone else to do something that you have not consciously chosen to accept as your obligation and if you are not moved in a current moment of newly looking to accept the obligation, then it is not your Responsibility and the most appropriate next step is to stop and ask of that other person why he or she believes otherwise.

Human history also recounts many moments like Jack Dawson's struggle for life to save the life of his Love. This may have been Jack's last intentional act. He ended his own life well used. Can it be that true Love includes the readiness to share this ultimate gift?

Aspects of Responsibility~ Performance

Next, if there are obligations of action that you have consciously accepted and have yet to fulfill, then this Tule's appearance is a requirement that you acknowledge that fact as a means for asking yourself what is standing in the way of your performance.

When doing so, be gentle with yourself. Examining your relationship with those activities that qualify as your Responsibilities and which you have yet to fulfill advances your awareness of how you are showing up for others. When you are looking in this way, be honest with yourself and welcome your physical body feelings.

A non-performance may identify a failure of sincerity or a place of great pain. Can you see that agreeing to perform a task and leaving out the doing of it identifies a stopping place? When this is true, the Tule is intended to carry that act of stopping into your full conscious awareness, because the honest awareness puts you more fully in charge of your immediate world and reality. The Tule is inviting you to take hold of it all in an active and purposeful way.

It is a heart of honesty and a further strength to acknowledge that your status in this situation might be motivated by your own fear. If you see this situation somewhere in your life, look more deeply at what is holding you back. Fear is natural. Overcoming it by choice is food for Love.

If you find yourself holding the strength to acknowledge a failure of sincerity on your part, which is a non-performance perhaps not rising from the feeling of having been hurt by another, you may appear indifferent. You might also be covering that indifference, even an intentional selfish indifference, with a pretense of unawareness. When this is true the motivation will likely be easier to see for those one or more others you are relating to than for you. When you can connect with one of these indicators, you will do yourself a great service to notice that you are merely facing your own fear. The bigger our fears may become the more fully they can fall, and the larger the gifts of Love they produce. Look at what will aid you in extracting yourself from this condition.

Remember that if you use your experience of this Tule to apply negative judgments to yourself for what you have yet to do, then you are misusing the opportunity and missing its gift. The Tule's purpose is the dispassionate looking that advances your conscious awareness. If you are moved to be judgmental with yourself around your own responsibilities, just stop it. Your emotional and spiritual energies are more successfully used as Refinement. Your physical energy is best used in action. Your physical-body feelings will be supplying meaningful guidance in this area.

Observing your unfulfilled Responsibilities is more tangible and real than merely conceptual. Be honest with yourself and allow the Tule's challenge that you communicate with those others to whom you may also owe that honesty.

Such an examination may also lead you to recognize that one or more of your Responsibilities are ripe for revising. Has something in relevant circumstances changed such that your consequent obligations must naturally also change? If this is true the Tule is the requirement to face the challenge to accomplish that change. Responsibilities arise in relationship and so the means by which revising them is accomplished is again a full communicative honesty, as best you are able. Is there something to say to someone in your work or personal life that you have been avoiding or newly recognize as necessary?

Aspects of Responsibility~ New Opportunities

After you have, to your own satisfaction, honestly examined the state of your existing

Responsibilities, use the appearance of this Tule to look at the question whether there are new Responsibilities offering themselves in your life. Is there an opportunity of expanded Responsibility waiting ready in your world? Is there a next larger task it is time to accept or to look for?

Aspects of Responsibility~ Accountability

Another element of the meaning of Responsibility is accountability, the readiness to be called upon to "answer for" your acts or choices. This is an element of maturity and depicted in far simpler terms by the following story.

The mother of two teenagers noticed that she was frustrated by a consistent habit she saw in the operating of both her children. Early on a Saturday afternoon she would ask of her daughter, "what are you and your friends doing tonight?" Her daughter would describe their plans. Consistently, however, those plans would change any number of times across the course of the afternoon and early evening and typically end up as something never previously mentioned before her daughter actually left the house.

In some situations this can rise from a fear on the teen's part to be Responsible for making a definite choice and sticking by it. This may show a reluctance to take the risk of being judged by others (her friends) as having what might turn out to be a bad idea. It is a good example of the challenge of being that can hallmark teenage years in the United States, the challenge to take Responsibility, to say what one wants and stand by that. To be accountable, willing to be acknowledged as the source of an identified unfoldment.

Again, the Tule offers the invitation to look at the places in your life now where you may rightly be facing the challenge to take new Responsibility. Look carefully, knowing that accountability comes with all new Responsibility.

Aspects of Responsibility~ Averting Blame

When considering the matter of Responsibility it is also easy to look to what we perceive to be the Responsibilities of others and to become judgmental. The common human tendency toward judgment is addressed in the following section describing the Contrast Tule. To be judgmental about the Responsibilities of another, however, is the dark activity of building the foundation for placing blame which is correctly addressed here, as an aspect of Responsibility.

This and all the Tules are invitations to look at the part that you are playing in your life, rather than anyone else's. Placing blame is an aspect of Responsibility because to place blame in another is to shirk personal Responsibility yourself or to deny holding it. So when you find yourself placing blame or whenever this Tule appears, recognize the invitation being made to both release any such judgmental thought and look instead at the opportunity offered by the circumstances to expand the measure of your own Responsibility.

When we are moved to thoughts of blame, we have already missed an opportunity of Responsibility. As suggested earlier, blame can tend to rise from the mistaken presumption of a right to require a particular result when we have shared Trust in someone else. It is important to stay aware that this discussion is about your individual emotional states around the matter of Responsibility, and not the contractual agreements we may enter into or the requirements parents may sometimes impose on children. It is a pitfall to use this view of Responsibility to examine your level of satisfaction around the performances of others. You would be serving yourself and those others far more fully by examining the quality of your own communication. To do so is to advance your own Responsibility, which is the point, to accept the stated challenge, rather than to push it off by being right about the failures of others.

Responsibility includes honoring the reality of your impact over what you may have believed to be your intent.

The Responsibility Tule, like any other, can also appear as an acknowledgment of your successful accomplishment in any of the areas discussed here. It may be a commendation for having successfully fulfilled one or more of your existing Responsibilities or for having taken new Responsibility, having made yourself accountable in some new way that you had not thought about or had not been open to previously. As always, what's present in the moment is what counts. You alone are the judge of this. Let the Tule, whenever it appears, be a reminder of all these issues.

Aspects of Responsibility~ Creative Strength

"We each hold full and exclusive responsibility for everything we individually experience."

"Forgive them for they know not what they do."

In our world predominantly ruled by the ancient concepts of participation-by-conflict these two quotes may seem radically shocking ideas to think of as other than philosophical, metaphorical, religious, naïve, or quaintly unrealistic. Every appearance of the Responsibility Tule is also calling you to look at what for the author is the first most basic lesson of metaphysics, your full Responsibility, best expressed as in the first of the two quotes above.

As pointed to above, who are you blaming for what today? How many people in your life today still populate your list of the unforgiveable?

Events occur. Absolutely all of the meaning of each for you is the product of your choice about that. That's the whole story. These are our lives.

Determination is an aspect of Responsibility. Attitude is an aspect of Responsibility.

Forgiveness is an aspect of Responsibility. Your ability to derive for yourself a powerfully constructed understanding of the meaning of forgiveness is an aspect of Responsibility.

In most simplistic terms, forgiveness is the solitary, personal, individual experience of the ability to look at any event, person, or set of seemingly harmful (to you) circumstances and derive by choice an understanding of meaning that finds you personally unharmed, knowing yourself larger than the damage or harm that was done. Where the subject is emotional harm you think done to you by another person, it is at worst the product of the fear or confusion of that other person, or both. Would it make it easier for you to get beyond your feeling of hurt if you accepted or looked to understand an awareness of that other person's fear?

Our reactive human minds that, when attacked, will fight or flee are operating from the animal component of our brains. The uniquely human component grants us the freedom of choice referred to here.

We are not invincible, yet we are each personally in charge of our emotional responses to the events around us. We are each entirely unique and some of us may be more emotionally strong than others. When we work consciously to shape the manner of our thinking we derive an authority and strength we might not otherwise have known if we had not found the idea of that ability. The Responsibility Tule is calling you to notice that idea, that ability, that freedom of choice to consciously shape and construct the reality of your own awareness.

When we do allow ourselves the idea of that ability, a door can open to personal strength that may very widely free us from an otherwise (perhaps actually non-existent) place in consciousness most frequently thought of as victimhood.

The eighth of the 12 steps of Alcoholics Anonymous calls the users to list people to whom they have done harm and to become willing to make amends. Alternatively, your list of the unforgiveable is mainly a list of the people you think have done you harm, a much easier list to deal with. It's highly likely that some on your list can come off with just one wave of your imaginary magic wand, because when you allow yourself to look at your own authority over your personal emotional experience, it is the most highly likely that the only thing present is you holding some grudge that may not even be sensibly logical or justifiable in any terms.

It might be that the other person did not do anything at all to cause you harm. If you think your grudge is justified, the Responsibility Tule is calling you at a prescriptive minimum to look at and construct whatever communication would complete the experience of upset for you and free you from the pain.

Many of the people on our unforgivable lists don't even know they are there, or if they do, they don't know why. You might be doing them some reactive harm you think you have a right to inflict, though it's far more likely that the only one being done the most, perhaps any, harm is you, because the full construct of your emotional experience is entirely of your own doing, fully within your own authority, even if you had not noticed that fact.

You might be thinking yourself harmed by something absolutely no one else knows anything about.

If you find this true the Responsibility Tule requires that you laugh at yourself.

Most importantly this Tule is welcoming you to recognize the creative power of you own authority and the fact that no one else is holding that power over you or preventing it to you. To hold this Responsibility, which is not a burden at all, opens grand, wide spaces of new emotional freedom.

Forgiveness used in this way is the grounding heart of creative strength. Living this view is one component of our human connection to the ultimate purposes of the universe specifically pointed to by the Tulcidious Tule.

Any person allowing themselves to think that the reality of forgiveness in the life of one or more others working to live this view would grant license to or for their own acts of bad faith (because of the dishonest thought that they can escape Responsibility) is misusing that other and the Tules. That person is also living a lie to deny truth, betraying themselves, good will, well-being, and the entire human world, while living in conscious contradiction of the pervasive character and force of the Love present throughout the entire universe of existence where any part of human reality can be known.

Aspects of Responsibility~ Apology

Apology is an aspect of Responsibility. Whenever the Responsibility Tule appears it is also calling you to look at where you have done harm to the others around you in life and whether or not you are ready to do your best to repair that harm.

The founding place in awareness on which the Tules are based is an obligation to see us all come to know ourselves as wholly well and in full possession of the ability to return ourselves to that state whenever we may lose track. The Divine (   ) can want nothing less. This obligation makes apology one of the most important human acts.

From this perspective there are two distinctly identifiable components in the nature of a genuine apology generally described as follows.

Apology is called for when we have done harm to someone else, for any reason, by any means, and have found both the willingness and ability to bring ourselves back to a place of healthy relationship with that other person or with our own sense of integrity, or both.

As you will know from reading about the Willingness Tule, it is highly unlikely that there is any possibility of this repair at all when we lack that willingness.

Apology also requires advance planning for honesty on our part. This means that we must choose in advance exactly what to say to that other person.

Choosing the exact words in advance is not necessary. Read on here to see what the Tules are saying <u>is</u> necessary.

A communication of apology can be delivered in person, by phone, or in writing. The first component is the acknowledgment on our part that we have done that other person harm. Think of an example, look at the following language and see which parts of it fits your circumstances~

I know that I have done you harm.
I may not have seen that then, but I see it now.
I am sorry for what I did and today I wish that had not ever happened.

The first of these three lines is absolutely essential to the reality of the moment, that we acknowledge having done the harm. On the second line, it can be possible that in a moment of doing harm to someone else, we may not have recognized that our act would be harmful. Affirming again now with words like this that we see we in fact did harm to the other person is good to repeat.

Regarding the third line, remember that we are engaged in this conversation first to admit and acknowledge that we are sorry. All speakers of English know the word, "sorry," and something about the idea of "saying you're sorry." In this context wishing now that the harmful act had not ever happened is what it means for an adult to be sorry. If we cannot say that we are sorry for the harmful act for which we know we are responsible, that we genuinely wish now that it had not ever happened at all, then we are not ready to make an apology and our words will not ring true for our listener.

I am sorry for what I did and today I wish that had not ever happened.

The second component of a genuine apology is the part that makes it real, the part that is calling us to be most true to ourselves, the part that is spiritually magical, the part that our struggles with willingness are ruled by, and the part that is the most fully freeing~

I promise never to let it happen again.

This promise is the key that makes a genuine apology into a component of honest truth. When we are not ready to make this promise, our apology is not real. We might be sorry, but sorry without this promise is only an admission of error, and unless we can state our best willingness to cleanse ourselves of the force within that caused us to do the harm by making this promise, then being sorry alone won't do any good.

Importantly, there is nothing about this form of apology that requires the other person's acceptance or approval. The only thing necessary is that we be ready to do our best to keep aware of and responsible for our promise in all our further dealings with that person.

We are promising not to do harm. The more promises occur in our world not to do harm, the better off we all will be. Most importantly, by making that promise, we are freeing ourselves. If the other person is not ready to forgive us, a thing we may not require, it doesn't matter. It is your sincerity that is freeing you in the eyes of Spirit. Nothing more can be required of you.

Individual conditions may rule particular circumstances to require repayments, perhaps of money, or compensation for physical damages done. Yet it is the emotional pain we personally feel for harms we have done, and the ugly judgments against ourselves that we free ourselves from by this form of apology.

The event and our sincere ability to make the reparative promise is doing very beneficial limitation to the common tendency to condemn ourselves for our weaknesses. Such weaknesses in past harms done to others become powerful events of teaching and freedom when we can use them in this way to fulfill the best of who we are for today and all the days to come.

> *"A burden is an old-fashioned, unattractive name for an opportunity."*
> This means that there is a home for purpose in Responsibility. Welcome the joy that offers.

Contrast

The nonagon symbol here is a straight-line display of the simple difference between dark and light.

Contrast, duality, opposites. Some believe that the quality of direct confrontation identified by the many dualistic pairs such as light and dark, hot and cold, right and wrong, serve to supply the primary, if not the only, means by which humans can perceive or accomplish any form of certain knowing. One of the major purposes of this Tule is to make the strong suggestion that this is an extreme, potentially destructive, and limited view.

Contrast, understood to be the examination of polarities, alive most commonly in a pervasive, speedy tendency toward the rendering of conclusions of judgment, is merely one of many means by which reality and human activity may be guided.

A major purpose of some of the most historically significant religious texts, at least as they have been used by many, is to provide guidance in understanding the basic differences between right and wrong. Many systems of law are expressions of this. For example, the American judicial process, by means of which all US laws are ultimately subject to testing, accomplishes its judging purpose only when two opposing parties are able and agree to participate by formally disagreeing. Is the plaintiff right and the defendant wrong? Or is it that the defendant is right, and the plaintiff is wrong? Or in what precise degree is the derived resolution mixed as between the two, and how?

Some believe such tools of judgment, which can be stark, are the ultimate means by which all human affairs are rightly guided. Perhaps this belief is so strong because those many early books and systems played a very large role in our striving toward completion of the civilizing effort in which humanity has been engaged all throughout its long history. And yet, when examining the efficacy of such potentially stark tools of judgment it is hard to ignore the fact that in common public affairs it may occasionally be the largest number who will always find some struggle or disagreement with every such resolution. We are billions of minds. Perhaps we hold as many differing views.

This situation raises both the question, is finality ever possible, and rightly gives us reason to question everything about the supposed rectitude of the hegemony of our conclusions derived by means of a commitment to the firmest rigidities of judgment as our final mechanism for deriving truth. Many courts and juries have been wrong. The emotional realities of the vastly many more personal lives of us all are far more soft and subtle than to maturely believe that a final act of complete condemnation can always be relied upon as a precisely correct means for deriving truth and communal wholeness. Today it may be more difficult than ever to think that such rigidity can be our firmest foundation. Perhaps we are more successfully served by the right encouragement of any efforts made toward themes of understanding and compassion.

To emphasize the point, the judgment process and the common tendency to rush to it, both within the full subtlety of human experience, are useful means for action, though this Tule exists in part as the reminder that they are only partially so. Today such rushing to judgment can fairly be described as providing only an incomplete utility, not giving us "the full picture," much like the difference between black & white and color television. Judgment in these terms is *one of many* tools by means of which human affairs can be and still are advanced.

I. Brain Growth

If we may also see our place in human history contextually, we may be able to think that the judgmental manner in our nature is a component of something that may have historically been an evolutionarily accomplished necessity for survival. Here the Tules are intended to remind us that they were created at the turn of the 21st century in part to help us see beyond both a seemingly innate tendency and the social limitations among so many traditions which were derived at times when both the gifts and dangers of technology as we know it today were in predominant part completely unknown and the measure of the population of today's Earth was likely unimaginable.

Here in the Lifeboat the treatment of judgment and its mechanisms, identifying them as aspects of Contrast, advances an important awareness by placing all such dualistic concepts and methods into a broader style of totalistic perspective which is more honestly consistent with life as we know it today. From the perspective of these Tules the role of the world's religions is rightly seen in that historical context which points our attention toward relationship with what we have most directly to revere: the commonalities of caring we know as families and our collective responsibility for humanity's relationship with the Earth itself.

Some use the opportunity of religiously founded forms of judgment to focus on conceptions around a strong sense of separated Divine (   ) action as both singular, absolute source to human existence and still also elemental somehow to deriving our final choices throughout all the questions and challenges that face us daily in human affairs. Can it not seem to lack intellectual, even emotional honesty to suggest that an unknowable force is rightly identified as our final ruler and judge when no one can speak for that force?

From the more tangibly immediate perspective of these Tules, our most meaningfully impactful focus is the advancing expansion of quality in and among our relationships in communities and with the planet, that common home that has been "mother and protector" to us all, the Earth itself. The concept for reasoning behind this conclusion is the view that these pursuits will most successfully affirm the accomplishment by humanity of the good in a functionally symbiotic relationship with the planet.

The invitation of all the Tules is to think for yourself and to understand the invitation of Divinity. This focus is the matter of how you use the attention you hold for your sense of the Divine (   ). More than to see that sense as ruling you with pre-ordained ideas, the gift and challenge of your awareness here is an affirmation of the depth of your acceptance of the immensity that is both your freedom to choose and the impact of your doing so, wholly irrespective of how we all got here to be that. You are living hands and beating heart in existence as form in a confluence that is all the universe advancing on to the awareness and understanding of itself. You walk, talk, live, act, and think with the full permission of the Divine (   ). You are a fully granted Creator. You are how, the means by which, that Divinity accomplishes its choosing. This Tule is also the reminder that moments of such choosing can be very small and always are fully creating acts.

The seductive simplicity of rendering the easiest, or speediest of final judgments, so common and readily accessible, resides, in the conception of these Tules, as important to hold largely passé because that seductive simplicity mainly points to a relative lack of committed care in a world of ever more subtle precision, intricacy, and worthy intimacy which remains largely inaccessible when we attach ourselves thoughtlessly or insincerely to easily derived or rigid conclusions. Such attachment can come off as showing an indifference on your part. To be consciously ruled by attachment to that seductive simplicity is laziness, perhaps even meanness. The purpose of the Tule in such terms is to carry your attention to the manner of your own thinking, particularly regarding your experience of others. Be honest with yourself. Be kind and bear this gift with honor.

If these ideas seem odd it becomes meaningful to consider the graphic representation of the Tao from Chinese philosophy, which reminds us that in all our experiences of the mutually moving dualistic energies of light and dark becoming each other, Yang and Yin, there is to be found the seed of the other, a subtle gift that reminds us to laugh at our own rigidities because not to do so may actually be impossible.

This take on Contrast and the Tao also supplies us conceptually with a means for understanding the presence in our consciousness of what may be called one elemental component of energetic being. The Contrast Tule offers the idea of a metaphorical awareness of ourselves that can be a source location, like a home, from which emotion and feeling states arise. Said another still metaphorical way, the tension that is the experience supplied to us by this understanding of Contrast, our tendency to judgment, is one home, or engine, or source "location" for feeling and emotion.

That derives substantive meaning because those among our choices that supply authority over our widening understanding of ourselves grant to us a style of benefit which makes us stronger as individuals. When you see the arising of this tendency in yourself, the Tule exists to remind you that you are witnessing a measure of your own strength and you are at full authority to find the welcoming presence in the partnership of all human consciousness, knowing that by doing so you will move with more than your individuality to the shaping of truth.

II. Context as Contrast

While we can all easily differ as to the level of conscious awareness we will attribute to the Earth, our collective progress has made it possible to understand our Earth as both expanding and naturally supplying a wide variety of means for our survival. Cognizance of this cannot be maturely trivialized. Whatever your strongest feelings in these regards may be, this Tule offers the view that all such considerations of context may also be fairly hefted as aspects of Contrast. We gain strength by affirming that whole. The Earth is a living thing, not merely a set, unchanging object, subject to your preferred conclusions.

When the Contrast Tule appears, it may mean that the time has come to finally resolve an important choice facing you. It might also be offering the opportunity of examining whether the means by which you currently make choices reside within a relatively limited perspective. Where this is so, the Tule is suggesting that you lighten up some by widening your readiness to be of welcome or ask again how honest you are being with yourself.

There may be no ultimately right answers to be found when considering our own issues or challenges and these Tules identify the idea that facing them matters. The Tules are intended to serve you in both identifying and understanding your own thought processes more fully and offering you a consistent means for opening yourself to new options within a clear and understandable framework.

If you can imagine yourself in a Lifeboat of survivors from a downed ship, the concept of Contrast is a way of offering you the warning that because you have now been thrown together with other individuals you might not have chosen in normal circumstances, it is appropriate to be prepared for the unexpected. Keep aware also that your readiness in this regard need not be a grant of license to others, though someone else might, in some challenging moment, choose to act as if it were.

Many of us live large portions of our lives comfortably ensconced in a tangible and clearly understandable way that is easy for us. Striving to achieve such comfort is natural, yet our comfort may leave us unaware that there are many other ways of nature and features of life the first experience of which can arrive in very stark Contrast to what we consider normal. A simple example of this is the difference between life on scholarship in a western style college and life in the working world. Another is the way in which calamity and illness can suddenly and unexpectedly change our lives.

Again, the appearance of the Contrast Tule includes the reminder to be ready to anticipate the unexpected. It also offers an invitation to consider the matter of what you most like and why. The appearance of this Tule may indicate that you are facing the possibility of a heretofore unexamined challenge. What do you see?

Naturally knowing that, careful and cautious discernment is also an aspect of Contrast. Daily life, as it faces you around what can be your most difficult individual decisions, may occasionally leave you finding a forceful positionality in the input of one or more others who are close to you, presenting a specific suggested path or resolution of your choice which that other describes as derived from the advantage of long experience. When you find such input shared by another with a forceful, unsought, authoritative manner, it becomes imperative both to listen most carefully and to look just as carefully, and likely more so, within. Any such forcefulness presenting a domineering "rightness" and shared by another, most particularly if it surprises you, requires your immediate attention at the fullest depth of your personal examining ability.

From the perspective offered by these Tules, this situation is calling you to discernment, one of your most useful human capacities, which can be defined both as "making out a thing with the eyes, as from a distance," and as "to detect or discover with other senses than vision, revealing insight or understanding, especially that which is hidden or obscure."

It is a major aspect of the purpose of this Tule to offer us all the permission for such discernment, particularly when we may be challenged to allow an important choice to be resolved by a force of any kind coming from outside ourselves. It is easy to allow ourselves to be ruled by a potentially rigid attachment to the dominance of an unexamined sense of obligation perhaps imposed by merely familiar practices or norms formed in the past and commonly presented to us through our cultures. While the seeming dictates of our home cultures may be derived from the advantage of long experience, whether it is right for your choices to be ruled in such a manner remains yours to decide. This is the key purpose of your life today in individual being.

All our lives are vastly more intricately featured now than ever before because of the new, rocket-speed progress of technology and the explosion of the world population which has supplied to humanity a state of circumstances we have never known or had to deal with before. This makes it potentially even more likely that the best voices of the past cannot be unthinkingly relied upon to hold the most appropriate definition of your next step. The appearance of this Tule is the admonition always to look for yourself.

This Tule is also the reminder that when we sit in individual judgment of each other, we prove our own hypocrisy. Where it may appear that such a view challenges some societal norms for setting up particularly identified adult persons to do exactly that sitting in judgment, it can fairly be suggested that such practices may be questioned as operating in a manner now outdated as less able to meet the needs of that societal intent than may have been sought.

Today such means can easily prove dangerously out of touch in the face of the desperation frequently brought about around both the immense complexity of our modern lives and the shocking level of girth in our human numbers. Most communities are not as small and familiar as they once were. For these purposes the Contrast Tule is also leaving us with the reminder to maintain a strong readiness to step back when we find ourselves in judgment of others (all issues of judgment around ourselves are matters of Refinement).

Respecting this view might be arguing the existence of a major structural flaw in some long established and revered norms of societal practice, yet denial of reality is not the point. Denial is the problem. Please look upon your individual circumstances in these regards with circumspection and honesty, remembering prominently that the Tules are calling you to a maturity in relationship with your own thinking, rather than the actions of others.

Remember finally that we miss the opportunity of possibility when we think there can only be one right way. Keeping ourselves reminded also that life is more than just black and white leaves us a far broader realm of possibility offering ready leaps in conscious awareness. In simple terms this Tule is also offering you the reminder not to rush to conclusions, perhaps instead to look a little more slowly and carefully when your personal tendencies might otherwise seem to be offering you a familiar speedy reactiveness.

Every feature or aspect of Contrast we get to know is an immensely useful mechanism for perceiving and discerning. You are being called to look on all of what you find there as a kind of metaphorical engine holding a deeper quality and potential than meets your immediate attention by means of the direct and present confrontation or conflict giving rise to your experience, whether that be derived in a human body experience or in the noticing of the same or in the noticing of some particular thought.

The author's response to the question, why is that meaningful, is the awareness of a clarity that where metaphysical conception can offer us opportunity we succeed the most fully when we allow such opportunities to supply the experience of knowing ourselves as agents for the derivation of truth rather than as ready proponents in some battle. In this sense you might allow yourself to think of the Contrast symbol as representing the doors of a cabinet opening onto a far larger reality than you had thought present or known visible and which you had not noticed could open at the mere direction of your readiness.

This barely visible component of the rush to judge another (the opportunity not to) might in fact be an offered awareness of something entirely different than what we had believed. The freedom to notice supplies source for your Nature as a creative actor, again affirming your reality as the hands and feet of Creation itself.

Contrast identifies a tendency which is one mechanism by which we may know the means to resolve our affairs. There are far many more.

Where some might find the reality of Contrast as calling conflict and confrontation natural or normal in human affairs, the author's intent is to have you know to include the importance, when this Tule appears, of ever remaining ready to choose for action, from among the many options just as easily within reach, that affirm resolutions without any confrontation whatsoever, or a winner and loser at all. The caring concepts of active, spoken communication, openness to collaboration, and bridge building are examples of manners of that kind.

III. Discernment

Your noticing of a mere difference is providing an example of the opportunity of discernment, already identified as an aspect of Contrast. This means also that when this Tule appears it may be pointing out the reminder that you are facing some simple, seemingly small, "difference of manner" with another person that is not normative in your experience or preference. It may be the challenge to acknowledge or admit that something may have shown up which has far more significance or substance than you have been willing to recognize until now. For example, an emotionally based denial of some kind. Perhaps a place of difficulty the stress around which has been so hard to acknowledge that you have lived either a self-blinding denial or a façade of unknowing indifference as though the matter has no meaning for you at all.

Sometimes we excuse in ourselves perspectives in thought or actions that can seem indifferent toward or to others, by falling back upon the explanation that, "I just see certain things differently than he (or she, or they)." This is a voice for your own fear that the Contrast Tule is challenging you to admit. Typically some fear of losing a place of safety which is protecting you from what otherwise would be an experience of honorable and natural vulnerability.

Opening to the risk of Being in such places of vulnerability is feeding Love. The Contrast Tule is inviting you to let go of your overly protective manner, your fear of losing whatever safety you may think is at risk. Are you being horrible toward someone else at a very safe distance? If so, the Contrast Tule is inviting you to let go and take the risk of opening to communicating instead.

As you will find the context of the Responsibility Tule reminding you, by the action of your rigidity in these terms, in kindest words, you are preventing yourself from the gift of truth. As always, your chosen conclusions are what rule your life here.

These suggestions can seem an extreme example, though that may merely be to remind you that such subtlety is present in every moment and form of relationship in our lives, not merely those places where we would define ourselves as being horrible toward someone else. Don't judge others. Speak with them.

> *"Contrast depicts humanity's primary ground of confrontation. We fail ourselves when allowing our manner in that terrain to cause us to do harm."*

Time

Time is a neurological sensate mechanism through which we define and understand events. The symbol in this nonagon is an hourglass.

As a mechanism, Time is a tool, just as the hourglass, the sundial, and the clock are tools. This Tule invites you to acknowledge that your experience of joyful events is impacted significantly by the way you relate to Time. When the Time Tule appears, stop to observe your own conceptions of Time.

Some people relate to life as though there isn't enough Time, even though some major religions and philosophies teach that you have or are an immortal (exempt from death) "soul."

Many believe we return to a new human body repeatedly until all our reasons for being in human life are fulfilled. This also suggests the presence of spirit (or soul), as an aspect of your Nature that is you, yet somehow more all-encompassing and real than the boundaries of the body you now occupy and the limits you perceive through what you understand to be the features of human life, including Time. Many believe we are spirits merely having human body experiences. Literature on what some call the "subtle body" and near-death events also depicts consciousness apart from the physical body.

If you believe your individual essence to be of spirit and if you believe further in the concept of free will, the independence to make choices for yourself, then you may be able to understand the suggestion that your presence here in human life is the result of a choice made by that larger all-encompassing essence that is your spirit. That is the choice to be in a human body, accessible to all the opportunities and subject to all the frailties which that may include, as well as all the other features of life on this planet, of which Time, as you experience it, is one.

Free will is an element of your intelligence. You have come here for a reason. Time is a tool that helps you identify your choice to be here as having a useful purpose.

If you can accept this conception of Time as a tool or skill we are somehow individually using, rather than as an element of reality we have no control over, then you may be able also to accept the suggestion that one of the prominent uses to which many humans put Time is worry. If you find yourself in the Lifeboat and turn the Time Tule, look within at the level of your worry and consider the ways you can release some of it and potentially expand your joy. Frequently this shift is merely a simple choice, to live in the moment.

Some think their available Time is a precious commodity defined by the measure of what remains between Rest periods after their Responsibilities are fulfilled. Others live to enjoy the moment by moment fulfillment of their Responsibilities, and much more. Could it

> *"All I have Time for is peace and joy."*

be then that to choose enlivening Responsibilities is one pathway to freeing yourself from the worries that come to life within your personal conception of Time?

The appearance of this Tule is a reminder to examine anew your individual experience of Time and the impact your relationship with it has on your daily level of happiness.

If you see yourself as "trapped" by Time, running out of it or struggling with it, the appearance of this Tule is an invitation to give the matter another thought. How do you use Time? How do you find yourself handling the upsets that occur for you around Time?

Addressing these questions may make available a greater sense of control over your level of happiness than you might otherwise have imagined possible.

Time in this perspective may also be viewed as a home for mathematics.

All questions have a home in Time. An example that makes this apparent is the question, "How much of your life have you devoted to what you most care about?"

If you were suddenly called upon to respond to that question, it is likely you might ask for some Time to think about it. You might also wonder why raising such a question is meaningful. These are two of the large questions that occupy the matter of knowing and clarifying who you are. Time might then also be said to be the existential home of permission.

Time exists in part so that Rest can be real. Finally here, Time in a three-word display~ Now, Then, When. Meaning full or meaning less, Time's up!

> *"Please don't be afraid. Time has the meaning you give it."*

Willingness

To be willing is to have the mind favorably disposed to doing some specified thing, not refusing.

The symbol in this nonagon is a raised hand indicating readiness.

Here we acknowledge the sadly obvious: nothing can constructively change in all human affairs if we lack the Willingness to allow it. Willingness is the foundation for all intentional change.

Willingness is the situation where all involved parties begin with a favorable disposition toward some identified change or resolution of a conflict or condition. Willingness hallmarks collaborative functioning, is achievable in all circumstances, and represents one of the foundations for an ethic in human affairs that most benefits all.

Need, bravery, self-discipline, and anything you see as merely relevant to you are all aspects of Willingness because they are all either motivated or resolved by it.

Desire is an aspect of Willingness.

Refusal is an aspect of Willingness. When this Tule appears, look at the prominent stopping places in your life. Examine the ways you use refusal and observe what you use it to protect.

Change in human affairs is not inherently imperative, but rather consistently inevitable. This Tule offers the opportunity to examine what part you individually play in the change that has potential around you.

Do you resist the changes that offer themselves in your world? The prime focus here is not a judgment about openness to change but rather the invitation to examine the level at which your relative Willingness impacts your individual happiness and the happiness of those others in the world of relationship around you.

Willingness is the means by which fear most frequently disparages itself. Fear is one of the primary foods of Willingness. This means that your fears come to life predominantly as barriers to Willingness. When you can see this is true in the circumstances of your daily life, you can surmount your fears by consciously advancing your Willingness, however gradually as you will. At a minimum, defined by your personal commitment to comfort.

Willingness then, as an aspect of that which degrades fear, identifies a home and ground for bravery. While much of culture and human history turned the idea of bravery into features of aggression or a qualifier defining virility, those ideas derive a limited, likely myopic perspective. Mere Willingness, viewed as a visible pathway or source for everything reaching even on to imagination, shows you a valuable challenge to step outside your common comfort zones. This Tule is inviting you to look at possibility in everything around you, notably including those places where your emotional, social, or actual physical survival might depend on your openness. Ideas have life. The appearance of this Tule is telling you to live your ideas with active engagement.

The accumulation of experience, previously described as food for Recognition, is possible because of your Willingness. You might not have survived if you had failed to be Willing. You might not actually have any idea of who you are if not for your Willingness.

> *"Willingness is home to consciousness."*

Ability

This nonagon's symbol is a sprouting seed. Ability is the potential within a seed, to open and sprout.

Ability is the skill, strength or personal emotional resources necessary to perform and is found frequently as either a natural aptitude or an acquired proficiency.

You are able.

You are an individualized expression of the nature of humanity. As such, you can bring about the accomplishment of anything humans can do. Anything that you can imagine doing, you can find the way to make real. You already possess all the tools you may ever require. Any tools you may lack, you know how to obtain. The appearance of this Tule includes the invitation to examine the degree to which you believe these things.

Doubt, in the form of any lack of confidence or questioning of yourself, is an aspect of Ability. Any self-doubt is fear that places you in the Lifeboat, and has you facing or engaged in questions of Ability. There is nothing inherently wrong with acknowledging doubt. The Ability Tule is also intended to remind you that when in doubt, a larger perspective offers you the challenge to recognize the opportunity to grow your own sense of Ability. Doubt then, is one of the foods of Ability.

Uncertainty, which is a lack of knowledge rising around any confluence of unresolved events, is a widely common human experience as well as an aspect of Ability. When you turn this Tule, look at whatever you may be dealing with that you are uncertain about. Remember that the uncertainty you may experience does not diminish your Ability. The Tule is offering you a challenge to examine what knowledge you may be lacking and how you might change that.

Every appearance of the Ability Tule is also offering the challenge to know and carry yourself as a consciously calculating engine for Peace. While your awareness will remind you of the many potentially destructive uses of your physical and mental ability, this Tule is calling you to recognize yourself as actively calming from that. Calming from the extremity of horrors and destructiveness so well-known and long resident in human physical ability. We all possess an evolutionarily derived reactivity, the fight or flight response, as a function of which we can tend toward a combative, competitive, or merely attacking responsive manner in our thinking and acting that may seem automatic and even generalized around all our activity.

That reactivity feeds a normative manner that in the least shows up as unimaginative, frequently careless, and even indifferent toward our undeniable surroundings in relationship with others.

Where Ability is the proving ground of the mind and well-being is an aspect of our Ability, you are challenged by this Tule to be the presence of a second thought that looks beyond those seemingly normative manners of reactivity toward the questions of yourself that can aid you in advancing understanding and the finding of common ground in all your experiences of others.

Ability is typically a function of what you believe to be possible and arises when your Willingness to make an effort exceeds the strength of those limits around possibility that you impose upon yourself. The limits you impose upon your own sense of the possible can otherwise substantially impair your Ability.

Extenuating circumstances such as a downed ship or other sudden emergency can sometimes result in our discovering Ability we may have long possessed but neither previously recognized nor had reason to bring to life. The same may also be true when an individually derived sense of either opportunity or a new personal choice for obligation carries us to a previously invisible sight within the limitless store Love grants as possibility.

> *"Ability includes the joyful fruition of imagination and is a source of individual fulfillment."*

Freedom

Freedom is the absence of necessity, coercion or constraint in choice or action. Freedom is unimpeded access to truth. The symbol in this nonagon is a bird in flight.

Just like the concepts represented by many other Tules, Freedom is relational. The appearance of this Tule is the invitation to examine both your experience of Freedom and the ways you impact the Freedom of others.

Today, at less than the most extreme, the first Freedom is the Freedom to define Freedom for yourself, with the single proviso that in living Freedom, one may not intrude on the rights, welfare, or Freedoms of others. One aspect of Freedom then, is that respect which prevents us from doing harm to others, all while the essence of Freedom remains access to truth.

Individual Freedom is the real foundation for all law because all law exists to protect it. Odd and basic as the idea may sound to state, Freedom includes the human Freedom merely to exist.

Any honest form of respect would then, of necessity, be a respect for all perspectives that do not license the doing of harm. Respecting the right to Freedom of all others will affirm your own Freedom the most fully. For this reason, it may be said that Freedom is the home of the obligation of honesty.

Freedom is how both privacy and choice are accomplished. The unimpeded right of choice is also at the heart of the nature of Freedom.

Any person who respects your right to think for yourself may fairly anticipate the ability to enjoy the same respect from you. For example, in the realm of the effort to understand ultimate questions of existence, we are each free to think for ourselves. In doing so we might each arrive, by using whatever tools we may individually have available to the purpose, at a genuine personal sense of clarity as to the nature of things, what one might call an understanding of ultimate reality. This is an aspect of the Freedom to think. Thinking about what the answers may be to ultimate questions is also an aspect of the Full Presence "state of being" known as Exploration.

One of the unfortunately repetitive practices vivid in the human way has been a concerted effort on the part of some to impose their individual or group understandings or views of ultimate realities on others. Doing so lacks respect for the reality of those others and constitutes a theft of Freedom. In many other realms of thought humans frequently make similar efforts to impose their personally derived understandings or views on others. This lacks respect, imprisons Freedom, and denies the legitimacy of both imagination and individual intelligence which are among the elemental pillars in the advancement of human civilization. Imagination is an aspect of Freedom.

A common theme among us is to strive for truth and many succeed at deriving an individual sense of what is true. Curiously, one of the lessons of some of the most intricate works of quantum science is that the mere act of observation impacts what we see. This suggests that deriving certainty about truth may sometimes be more complicated than is easy to admit.

Our striving for truth may merely be an understandable and natural striving for a sense of security. Choosing an individual understanding of the nature of truth is a right that for many resolves this striving. Many others prefer to refrain from all necessity to find firm ground, gaining a sense of truth instead from a resolved absence of knowing, or from a complete unconcern about security. This is a right it is an aspect of Freedom to live.

What that means is that if you believe in your own Freedom, you have an obligation to respect the rights of others to believe as they do and to be free from the violence that might likely come to life in the imposition of your view. Welcoming open communication can always make these reaches easier where our Freedom meets that of others.

The variety of possible views of truth capable of being pointed to in words of this kind may be infinite. While looking at truth as a function of Freedom, it becomes possible to see that a tendency or drivenness toward or attachment to fear in many human manners can make visible a confusing by some of their beliefs with their very definitions of truth, even reality. Individually this is the question, how honest are you being with yourself? Beyond that, are you being honest with others? Any lack of honesty on your part is an impairment of Freedom.

These subtleties are the work of the emotional which is an aspect of your human body experience. Fear plays a part in any lack of clarity around your sense of honesty. This is a thing to be guarded against where your beliefs derived from fear may be unfairly allowing you unwarranted license to impose your views of truth in the lives of others around you. To do so is aggression, destructive of Freedom. Where you understand a challenge in these words, your operating may be motivated by any variety of forces encircling the basis of your honesty that have yet to be fully examined. For the well-being of us all, please look.

The treasure in your sense of clarity around security might be of no meaning whatever for your neighbor, may even have no meaning or access to truth whatever beyond your own conclusions of purpose and intent. Be respectful in the way you spread your treasures of particular clarity around.

Freedom is Love under all conditions.

> *"Your freedom only defines mine as far as mutual respect honors us both."*

The Vibrations of the Earth

The progression of experiences depicted by The Vibrations of the Earth supplies a firm roadbed for understanding human nature through the concept of mere being. They offer an awareness of the very coming into existence of our Earth home, not in the form of a narrative story, but as the opportunity of an experiential knowing of what is best described in human terms as a birthing.

The seven Vibrations Tules are identified here in the specific order in which the author originally experienced them~

Gravity, A Wave Within
Unthinkable Pressure
Multitudes Beyond Imagination
Exposure
Insanity
Trust Yourself
Love Yourself.

Each of these seven Tules has seven sides. A seven-sided object is called a heptagon.

These seven Tules are the reason that the information offered in this book stands secondary to the reminders that the physical objects of the Tules themselves are. The Tules are tangible reminders to look within yourself as an entryway to interacting with and knowing your own unique and innate connection to a vastly wider consciousness that is life. The gift of this progression of experiences, identified by the Vibrations of the Earth, provided the structural context that carried into existence the remainder of the Tules and their basic division into the two distinct groups of the Lifeboat and Full Presence.

In consequence, the Vibrations are rightly understood as the foundation for everything about how we may take in and make use of the Tules. They are depicted in the layout display at the bottom of the image to offer a visual connection to the concept of foundation.

As stated above, it is most precisely accurate to view these seven Tules as depicting the birth experience of our Earth home. Their utility in human consciousness resides in their ability to help us conceive of the immensity of the nature of force itself. A respect for the Vibrations can carry you to a real experience of boundlessness.

That sense of boundlessness and the opportunity of knowing yourself as having a grasp of limitless extent are inherent in the first five of the Vibrations. A more nearly human fiber, like a grounding in peace and strength, comes to life in the last two: Trust Yourself and Love Yourself.

Collectively, these Tules are an invitation to consider consciousness on an Earth-large scale and they offer a means for relating your individual humanity to that massive a reality.

Survival of all of the most immense extremities offered by the Earth-birthing process, at least as lived by our Earth, is yours and offers you the polite, relatively easy, but just as immense experiences of both Trusting and Loving Yourself as the fulfillment of that "process." Trusting Yourself becomes your first breath, Loving Yourself~ your first meal.

Your "life" may be perceived as a reality that need never end. In individual human terms, you are full, whole, and well. You can handle anything.

Gravity, A Wave Within

Among the first most vivid realities we all know as humans in relation to our Earth is the experience of Gravity. The symbol in this heptagon is three arrows pointing down to a ground that appears flat.

This is the first of the Vibrations of the Earth, the Earth's first Voice. If you will imagine being the Earth you might recognize that you would probably experience the reality of Gravity as a wave that goes inward, perhaps like an inhaling.

This experience suggests a course of coming into existence for the Earth that somehow began as a location for a gravitational reality to gather or understand itself as aware, and hence found. The first humanly describable character of that experience is as an inward moving wave.

Our hearts are pumps that are in part pushing our blood in an outward direction, in waves impelled by each beat, in order to move it throughout our bodies. The Earth's own experience of Gravity is like that but of the opposite direction. It is that form of movement, that other component of our hearts' work, experienced as a wave that proceeds inward rather than outward, in human terms returning the blood to our hearts. In this realm of relational realities, that Wave Within is viewed as the first form of sensual nature for the Earth. Imagine that inward moving wave as very gentle. You already know its constancy.

Your weight is an expression of the simple constancy of that wave. That gentle inward moving wave is the Earth's heartbeat. That's Gravity, A Wave Within.

Respect for the idea of partnership with yourself (your awareness and your presence) is an aspect of Gravity. Beyond the Vibrations this form of respect may be known to occur in the Lifeboat, visible as meaningful in Time.

In human terms, the appearance of the Gravity Tule also offers the challenge to acknowledge the undeniable features of your fundamental daily life reality, which includes the gradual unfolding of the experience that something larger has occurred and, nonetheless, you have hold. It is also an invitation to consider the possible malleability of those elements of your life that you view as the most unchangeable.

> *"Your relationship with both choice and sound are aspects of Gravity."*

Unthinkable Pressure

The symbol in this heptagon is three inward pointing arrows surrounding a circle of focus, which is you.

Distinct from Gravity, this is a multi-directional pressurizing into a great stillness. A level of pressurizing to stillness so full that it is beyond your imagination to conceive and beyond the limits of words to describe. Even unthinkable.

When the wave of Gravity accomplishes its task of pulling inward and carries everything that became the Earth to the end of what must be known as a natural path, there remains the product of that unimaginable, beyond your ability to conceive, inward pressure, a pressure so full it produces nothing other than absolute stillness.

Arising amid this, your normative essence is only able to recognize itself as thinking, though not able to think outside this Pressure. You have been removed from the movable. The experience is not within your thinking ability to define, describe, understand, or surmount with thinking on any terms. Some subtly arising sense of terror can accompany the moment, though this Pressure remains so predominantly intense as to prevent even the movement of your attention in such directions. Astounded, you are merely alive.

Imagine now being rock. If you appreciate the utility of Meditation, go to your fullest guided-meditative state and allow yourself to imagine being rock. Then leave yourself there for as long as it takes to allow the experience through all your chakras or any other formative elements of Self that you know. The result can begin as frightening yet is fulfilled as a beautiful stillness because, within it all, you still breathe.

That breath is one of The Vibrations or Voices of the Earth. Its name is Unthinkable Pressure. It is Pressure beyond the measure of your ability to conceive.

You are rock and you breathe, wholly formed, raw, new, unspecialized, complete, and within it all fully well.

Multitudes Beyond Imagination

The symbol in this heptagon is the horizontal figure-eight typically used to represent the idea of infinity, with what appears to be an escaping, arrow-pointed arc.

Multitudes Beyond Imagination is a complement to, though distinct from, Unthinkable Pressure. See them as two faces on the same coin. At their core meeting point, they are intimately similar experiences, yet described separately so that you can know them in their correct nature as distinct, one progressing from the other.

Multitudes Beyond Imagination identifies the birth of perceptual specialization following the Unthinkable Pressure that only accomplishes the absolute maximum capable of being pressed into the reality of a single individual. This is the start point of the birth of consciousness. Following everything physical existence could put upon you at once this is the moment beyond which that is unbearable.

The perhaps unrecognizable component of joy for this event of flowering is relatable to something like the big bang. A certain possibly unimaginable press into complete ruination immediately upon perception, very suddenly exploding into a multitude equally beyond imagination, yet at least tentatively supplying some minimal sense of relief, as living awareness. In human terms, this is the place we come to when meeting the inescapable undeniability of individual being. As such,

Multitudes Beyond Imagination supplied to the author a form of event in experience that can be called conscious transformation.

The overwhelm of experience in awareness this supplies is most easily relatable to the idea of counting. Metaphorically then, to hold Multitudes Beyond Imagination is to know yourself as one who has successfully counted (by somehow knowing) all the snowflakes that have ever fallen on the Earth throughout all time. Also, you have succeeded at counting all our Earth's grains of sand, all the places in space, and all the leaves that have ever fallen and ever will.

You have fully experienced infinity in every knowable way within every realm of thought or experience where that concept has any meaning at all. You have counted everything that will meaningfully yield itself to counting. You've done it all a number of times, over and over, beyond a countable number of times.

After learning about the concept of Unthinkable Pressure, you will be able to conceive of the arc of this symbol as not proceeding out into the unknown Multitudes, but rather delivering them to you. Here you are given a first experience of specificity, as the variety of Multitudes distinguish themselves from components of the mere Pressure that they might otherwise collectively comprise.

Just as Unthinkable Pressure offers a fullest experience of raw force played upon you, up to and not beyond the point of destruction, Multitudes Beyond

Imagination supplies to you the means to know as part of your Nature all of what that pressurizing can have arisen from, now as mere, raw possibility.

When you allow your awareness into all of that, you will know the experience as a form of strength, and a first home of vision.

Unthinkable Pressure and Multitudes Beyond Imagination are a direct pathway to unraveling an experience of the Infinite. This is one doorway to thinking about an understanding of what some scientists have referred to as the larger "Metaverse" within which the universe we know, and many others, can be said to reside or have resided.

You are invited specifically here to let your imagination run wild through the idea of counting, though you are beyond counting. You know yourself as counting itself. Allow yourself into the real experience of infinity as best you can imagine it. One aspect of your human life is a wholly inclusive transcending through a containing, knowing, holding, and surmounting of all the Multitudes of limitations that life can supply. Multitudes beyond your Imagination.

This Vibration breeds the Freedom and Ability to heft and manipulate infinite possibility.

Multitudes Beyond Imagination includes a connection that makes possible knowing the use of every perceptual experience you may ever hold.

Knowing the experience Multitudes Beyond Imagination includes the strength supplied by connection to an individual awareness of every particular desire, emotion, observation or awareness ever known or lived by every human who ever has or ever will walk this or any other planet.

Your awareness of the concepts represented by this Tule is an element of fully knowing its complementary Tule, Unthinkable Pressure. Here you understand all of infinity-aided pressure as brought to bear upon you, within all of which, by some natural means, you have produced for yourself the ability to specify all of Pressure into Multitudes so vast, beautiful, and natural that, within it all, you remain whole and well.

In human experience we can look to the world of books and notice that the early history of human writing produced more than one immense accomplishment of words intended to offer guidance for human lives. It may not be possible to recount by number every human thought that rose from and continues to rise from just some of the written works of human history, and yet we all stand, alive nonetheless, in the midst. The potential incomprehensibility of these realities is an aspect of Multitudes Beyond Imagination.

> *"You are rock, and you breathe."*

Exposure

The symbol in this heptagon is a stark outline of the human form, a reminder of the specific nature of your current existence, exposed.

Imagine now being mere fulfilled conscious existence. You are wholly round, a stone, like a marble, but with the soft skin you know now. Feel the growing, pleasureful warmth of the sun and the simultaneous coolness of a gentle breeze. A speck of sand blown by the wind touches your face and flies away. You are comfortable, at peace. Still. Alone.

Next, everything about this experience grows, ever so gradually. The sun's heat increases, eventually to the point where it burns through all the protection you can muster. The cold caused by the wind rises to meet the heat. The flying sand turns incessant, until it is wearing away at your surface. Continually and relentlessly you are being burned and frozen and blown and pelted, being worn away to something approaching nothingness.

You are eventually reduced to the measure of a single, meaninglessly small, molecular-sized grain of sand which is finally broken, blown away by the wind, and burned out of existence simultaneously with unmeasurable heat and cold. It is the fullest knowable devastation, yet somehow your conscious essence remains. You are alive, thrive, and survive. That's Exposure.

Exposure accomplishes a cleansing. When this Tule appears, welcome the level at which you can accept that cleansing. This is the birthplace of acceptance.

As a cleansing experience, the appearance of the Exposure Tule also invites your attention to the inevitabilities within the systems of relationship of which you are a part and suggests your examination of the feeling states that come with that.

The indifference of others is an aspect of Exposure.

The Exposure Tule also suggests you examine the level at which you allow yourself and your emotions to be known among those around you.

In addition, examine the impact that doing so has in defining your level of satisfaction with life as you have given it to yourself until now. Success in looking at these issues is accomplished by maintaining an observer's style of awareness while also acknowledging your presence both in and as the life observed. You are larger than all the issues and realities you face. Staying aware of this fact places those realities more fully within your control and authority.

As with all the Tules, the purpose of the examination is to support your individual sense of wholeness. When you acknowledge the seemingly hard realities you face in terms of what others may "know" about you, or how they may choose to operate in relation to you, your attention upon this Tule serves the purpose of aiding your comfort by offering the reminder that within it all you are still more fully in charge of the circumstances than everything outside yourself.

Intelligent maturity can gain strength and peace by such means.

> *"Living Presence hallmarks the wholeness of Love."*

Insanity

The symbol in this heptagon is one black tear.

You were fully exposed into nothingness (like being burned up in a fire, only more fully destroyed) and, having survived, you became completely insane. Today we know this too as an experience you escaped and survived.

Though not before you were rendered deranged, unable to speak, unable to call for help, unable to organize thought or make sense of reality, unable to remember, unable to proceed, unable to function, unable to move, unable to plan, unable to dream, unable to rest, and yet unable to die.

You were petrified by the experience, stunned into helplessness and hopelessness by all external perception, also sure that all accusing eyes were upon you in the fullness of the most widely and destructively negative satisfied conclusion that you were alone and personally responsible for hopeless failure. Every worst fear you ever imagined had come to pass, along with many you might never have imagined.

When this Tule appears for you, the meaningful focus is the fact that you survived, and that all of that is now mastered by you and gone. You are here with us to help us all speak more fully among ourselves about as much of it all as we can manage, for life, as fully as Love will allow.

As an example, some of humanity's survivors who have been to war prefer to refrain from speaking about their experiences. Many war veterans live with a knowing that no one else need ever be familiarized with what they have seen, lived through, known. These immense beings live like the locks on doors never to be opened because they know there is nothing to be gained by sharing what their eyes and hearts have known. For some such sharing is essential. For some it is pointless.

As a component of the birth experience, Insanity is the first home in this depiction of consciousness for fear. You survived the complete destruction by Exposure because there was no such thing as fear. With Insanity there is such a thing. Insanity is the home of fear. Fortunately for you, you are with us to read this because you survived the Insanity of your fear. It's OK to let you know that before you're taught how because Insanity gives to all forms of fear. Reading this you get the jump on that.

The result of your human connection to these forms of awareness is a transformative strength. It is as though your skin was surgically sliced up into ribbons, doctors poked around, pushing your organs from here to there, discarding this one, adding that, then sewed you back together, the sutures held, the medications wore off, the scars affirmed, and you returned to the functional living. You are whole, yet vastly wiser, a great gift of maturity and wellness for us all.

The purpose of Insanity as an aspect of your adult examination of the experience of birth is to extinguish attachment. You will know this is true when you see the freedom to laugh at yourself.

The primary component of meaning present in the appearance of this Tule is a welcoming to move more slowly. You are a full, whole survivor, accomplished, not beset.

Be gentle with yourself. Move on.

> *"You are ever still more than the worst of your experience."*

Trust Yourself

To Trust Yourself begins with accepting the reality that there is nothing to fear. To Trust Yourself includes acceptance for Self.

The symbol in this heptagon is the face of the Self, contained in most basic ways to affirm the formation of identity and confidence. Choosing this stance, to Trust Yourself, provides the clearest vision of human existence throughout all humanly knowable awareness and space in this earthly plane.

After knowing the likely horror of the first five Vibrations, it is in the outset of this, the sixth, that you receive the awareness that you have already survived a first-consciousness experience of Gravity, followed by a level of Pressure adequate to prove your resilience as more firm than diamond status (assuming accurately that you were already as hard as rock), that you then successfully received that pressure well enough to master it by transmutation into a multiplicity of acceptance beyond an infinity of identifiable conceptions, that you next survived a destruction into nothingness, yet lived beyond suffering any and all of the worst possible results that still surviving such an experience might mean.

You survived all of that. Congratulate yourself and begin to look around just outside your skin, recognizing that you are whole, in every way. A name for believing and living in this experience is Trust Yourself.

To Trust Yourself includes full readiness to go with your own advice when it conflicts with that of any other, even those others you already most fully Trust. The choice to do so is living that Trust. To Trust Yourself.

Certainty is an aspect of Trusting Yourself. Certainty doesn't make you right or define truth. It just helps to define you as someone who Trusts Yourself.

To Trust Yourself includes believing that you can make successful decisions in every aspect of your own life. It doesn't mean unrealistically thinking you know everything, though it does mean understanding that you are capable and know how to get any information that may seem to be lacking when you need to make an important choice.

What some refer to as "following your bliss" is an aspect of Trusting Yourself.

You know how to act in the face of lack. You know how to get what you think you need and how, who, and when to ask for help. Your physical body feeling state will always guide you in this way. A modern novel that depicts the Sixth Vibration is Sue Monk Kidd's, *The Secret Life of Bees.*

To Trust Yourself includes allowing the unfolding of respect for you by others and by yourself.

To Trust Yourself is the foundation and source of the Full Presence Tules which exist as a voice for all your creative ability. In this view all the Full Presence Tules are a product of Trusting Yourself.

The perspective from which the Tules arise is based in a framework of Ethics, specifically as distinguished from Morality. In this conception Ethics is viewed as founded in a respect for those rules of rightness derived through the long experience and works of humanity, though not divorced from either living voices or the honest benefits of your personal experience. Alternatively, Morality is seen here as limited to relying only upon those rules of rightness founded in the guidance supplied by what may be imposed or isolated conceptions of the Infinite Divine ( ) or traditional yet unexamined forces of culture.

The reason for this view is the belief that strength in the advancement of relationships is most affirmed by that consistency in human affairs rising from examined common experience rather than deeply rooted historical views more likely founded in times of authoritarianism.

We live here as the hands, hearts and minds of all the impressions of the Divine ( ) both able and willing to allow our continued existence. If there is some single Divine Being ( ), does it not stand as logically correct that such a Being ( ) would be enthusiastic to see our bringing into daily-life existence all the best we can, by using our received faculties to their fullest? Would such a One ( ) not encourage us and find joy in seeing our enthusiastic Willingness to Trust ourselves?

Is it possible that Trusting in ourselves and collectively in each other is a primary component of our given human task? Can it be that Trusting Yourself may also make it easier to Trust others, leading to healthy relationships and a wider field for happiness in general?

In addressing all the questions you may have found or may ever find in this book, when you lack any guidance stay aware that while the field of life is relationship, it can also be said that you are ultimately alone in being, even though all your choices still nonetheless have an impact in the totality of consciousness that is us all.

Please then always look to choosing in the manner that respects an ethically good solution. That you will do so is the final intent of this book. How you can begin making that easier will be seen in the next section.

> *"Rest in your awareness that you know how to do what's required."*

Love Yourself

The symbol in this heptagon is a heart, containing again the face of the Self.

Loving Yourself includes giving to yourself every fiber of kindness you have ever known or dreamed could be. All of compassion. All of friendliness. All the caring that allows you to recognize your own needs. Absolute self-acceptance, tolerance, and forgiveness. All you are that serves your personal ability to exist and survive as the advancement of Love in any level of honest happiness short of selfishness in relationship. All the best of everything you have ever thought, dreamed, or imagined about how a happy, mature and gentle kindness would share itself with others, granted first to yourself. This is motionless activity about which you need not ever speak with anyone.

You are giving life to all that supports the genuineness of being, residing at the heart of who you are. To Love Yourself occurs prior to stepping forth into relationship with any other persons or circumstances at all. Successful connection to the awareness this Tule depicts rightly is the foundation of your personal ground of being, even of your very existence.

To Love Yourself also includes politely releasing support for all you are aware of that does not fulfill the very best of who you are, consistently averting both self-destruction and any activity productive of harm that might be done to others.

Accepting the reality of this state of consciousness does not mean that you prove truth but does reaffirm the reminder to see yourself as standing whole.

From the perspective of the Earth's birth, Loving the Self resulted in the existence of the atmosphere that sustains all the life on and around our Earth's surface. And although the Earth's continuing act of Loving the Self can be called the source of humanity's ability to survive on the planet (and so, here may be seen as the foundation and source of the Lifeboat group of Tules experience), it is not the source of human existence on the planet. In this conception the source of human existence is to be found at the meeting point between the second and third Vibrations, represented by the Tule, Multitudes Beyond Imagination.

To explain, one of the opportunities occurring when this Tule appears is made more apparent upon your calmed understanding that what's being called for is something you've already been through, during your emotional birth, in the spark of life moment at the depths between, among, within, and rising around your advancement from the second Vibration, Unthinkable Pressure, to the third, Multitudes Beyond Imagination.

Specifically, though the events you are dealing with may be a wholly unknown experience, you nonetheless do already know how to do what is being called for in yourself. This is the opportunity or challenge of respect for yourself in every new moment. What matters is that you already know you are larger than your worst fears. For this reason, to Love Yourself includes the fullest intimacy with every part or place in yourself you have not wanted to face or touch, particularly those where you currently most find pain. An important strength rises for you here. The choice to know yourself as a conscious actor also means that you are finding the naturalness in granting permission to yourself. The Tule, Love Yourself, is a reminder of the birthplace in consciousness for this form of choice.

Pema Chodron is a modern author who has written beautifully from a Buddhist perspective to describe some features of this distinction and its rising occurrences. An elemental context for being, in the character and the quality of experience you are called to by the choice to grant permission to yourself, will be found in an understanding of yourself as a consciousness always making the choice as between means of communication that evince your readiness to step outside yourself with expressions that forward compassionate, caring Love or those that lead you to the communicative silence and worse that hallmark your fear.

Inside this perhaps incomprehensibly broad contextual viewpoint from which the Tules resulted, it proves wise for those setting policy in human affairs to remain aware of the importance of this distinction.

If you accept the idea that the Earth itself has a consciousness and intelligence of its own, and if you can accept the perspective on that consciousness and its origin presented by these Tules, then it becomes meaningful to recognize and understand that sustaining human life is not an act of Loving the Self for the Earth, but rather an act of Trusting the Self. The Earth doesn't need us.

At the level of the individual human perspective, remember first that Loving Yourself is the single act that most sustains your existence and sources your happiness.

The experience of Loving Yourself is elemental to being, as reality is relationship. You are knowing all these things as an advancement in the understanding of your own birth experience.

The resultant expanding personal private awareness of conscious strength is an aspect of Loving Yourself. Be kind, care, and live beyond doing harm.

> *"Your reality may only be a function of your conclusions."*

End Words

There are many ways of looking at and using these Tules. While they may welcome the passion in a reader's emotion and may even make you acutely aware of the differences between your own culture and those of others, the Tules exist so that you may see in yourself how to advance the beneficial openings that will move all humanity to a wider sense of collective success in affirming the well-being of all the life of this planet.

Allow yourself to use the Tules in every way you can see that your personal sense of caring for yourself, living relationship, and respecting the Earth will allow. They are intended to be an opening doorway out beyond the normal dimensional ways of thinking that we are all familiar with.

They offer infinity unraveling itself as an aspect of purpose through the thinking human mind and feeling human heart, unfolding what it holds within for you, and through you for us all.

As one specific example, consider the possibility that the Tules are offering you an invitation to re-contextualize your emotional states. They welcome you to look upon all your experience from a ground of being of fullness and a sense that all is well. You can let all your feelings be while knowing them now through a new kind of doorway to personal understanding opened by the concept of Full Presence.

The room behind the door each Tule opens has the distinct quality defined by the name on that Tule, and each of those rooms is boundless, opening out upon full permission to you as the hands and heart of Creation itself.

In Love All Ways

First Lessons Derived, 2020

This work is important to understand as abidingly secular. It is perhaps obviously derived from energies and experiences of human life. Its author respects the Divine as Love entirely. At a meaningful level, to do so is an actual activity of occasional and deeply engaged individual and personal requirement. These facts have made any serious consideration of this work controversial for establishments around the long and difficult history of all humanity. By that nature, the human faces in your experience of these understandable complexities are consistently essential to meet with compassion and understanding.

You are being told by this work that you individually hold permission and authority as a living agent of Creation. This state of permission to create is a part of the Divine ( ). We are each a part of our Universe, unfolding and discovering itself, and perhaps very much more. Your Nature holds a wholeness of being, around which you are completely at choice as one set of the motive, active, hands, mind, and heart of that Divine ( ), bringing itself forth as all the functioning process of consciousness you are, a human individual in relationship with the Earth and all its family.

By virtue of that nature, the character of human intelligence, and the great depth of such a granted and stated discovery, this work exists. Please examine it seriously. It is honest and responsible to consider the place of Tulcidious in your life after reading this book entirely. The text is both verbose in places and deeply brief. Please let this peculiarity make Tulcidious interesting for you.

I.
Creation as the Nature of Choice

The Vibrations of the Earth are to be seen as an allegorical representation of a series of events completed at the time of your birth by which you were granted the freedom and permission to both Trust Yourself and Love Yourself, as birthrights! Both reside within the true, living character of your Nature. That is so irrespective of the level of your specific awareness. This means that as you grow and allow yourself into these realms of permission, you will see potential actions resident in necessities of bravery to accomplish by not doing harm. These typically seem to be places of risk. As you take those risks, you may find a kind of welcome granting you a sense of expanding naturalness. When you do, rest in that welcome. It is a reminder that you have become more of yourself. The risks nonetheless are real, and they live visible as risks to remind you to operate with a careful caution, as they can also come across as experiences of others not easy at all.

The ideas represented and embodied in the Tules, Trust Yourself and Love Yourself, are two major themes that have not been prioritized in very much of human culture until now. They are also not at all unknown ideas. The distinction derived by the author's intent is to call your attention to the line drawn in your awareness between acts that do harm and acts that do not, where the latter are to be affirmed as that genuine Love resident at the heart of your being.

The easiest and perhaps both most well-known and most difficult example is the story of the words of the famous Nazarene, at the time of his crucifixion, where he is quoted as having said, "Forgive them for they know not what they do." In the sense present here, he did not "die for your sins." His intent was to share what example the yielding of his life could be. History has made a grand example of all his choices for action which led to that day and it is by that example this author believes that Nazarene rightly lives in the revered state so many hold for him even still today.

A cursory examination of the story, interpolating now to what he might possibly have intended then, leads this author to suggest that it is unfair, even verging upon dishonest, to suggest more. It has been said that he was able to accomplish certain miracles because of a state of well-being he could <u>Know</u> present in another (faith?) which, with his awareness, could not allow for the continued existence of infirmities such as blindness or a "withered" hand. In today's terms, can it be said that he held an enlightened state of awareness, making it possible to <u>Know</u> somehow that the combination of his clarity and the faith in that other could bring non-existence to the infirmity?

Can it also be said that he was crucified as the consequence of his arrogance, that extremely controversial arrogant awareness? If so, then it would be fair to say in a very beautiful way, that he gave his life willingly, if perhaps reluctantly with a sense of necessity, because others objected to and would not tolerate so many things which, in his own reality he <u>Knew</u> to be true.

You know what it means to stand firm for your own views. Recorded human history is replete with examples of the bravery of individuals giving their lives for their views. When was the last time someone hit you across the face and you turned the other cheek to them, risking further aggression rather than responding in vengeance?

What can it possibly mean to "die for" someone else's sins when sin is an idea you taught yourself and your own "sins" did not exist until sometime after you were born? If someone else "died for your sins" long ago does that mean you hold no responsibility for your own bad acts today? In the perspective described here, where sin is something you believe in, you complete the experience of your own sins for yourself. The Nazarene's intent was to be a good example for you, because he knew and said that if you could believe in his example you could do even greater things than he had. This author believes his inspiring character fully real. The better angels of our Nature have proven that character true.

How you relate to these ideas may be a reasonable measure of your personal sense of bravery and will certainly help to derive for you what you may believe creation to be. Every moment all the time the opportunity of creation remains open to your choice for conscious action.

You are that creator and Tulcidious is displaying for you means by which you may find, choose, and hold that status, knowing yourself as an affirmation of well-being. This is the meaningful focus. The author's intent is to advance the good faith strength in your thinking process. In that sense the intent of Tulcidious is directed more toward the character of your being as rendered by the manner of your thinking, than anything about what your specific choices for action may be. You will also find this work very much affirming the reality that your actions and your experience are entirely matters of your own Responsibility.

II.
Contrast & Refinement

The Lifeboat Tule, Contrast, describes itself in part as identifying humanity's primary ground of confrontation. A major component of this is the common character of the tendency to use means of judgment and discernment to derive your individual guidance. The section describing the Contrast Tule is written to encourage your attention <u>away from</u> works, activities, choices, and thinking that can reasonably be anticipated to do harm, all in a world where some few spend their days nonetheless deriving exactly how they shall.

You may find that the Contrast Tule is challenging your judgmental operating and it is important to read that section carefully to look seriously at your own manner whenever that Tule may appear for you. This reminder exists to emphasize one call mentioned only briefly in that section, that matters and energies you use in tending toward self-judgment are utilized more particularly and correctly as the energetic stuff of Refinement.

The interest you may possibly hold in understanding and deriving conscious attention for metaphorical concepts and their uses is an individual concern. Such concepts are best assessed by their usefulness to you. Before one is familiar with the specific distinction identified above, these "matters and energies tending toward self-judgment" can rise, perhaps obviously, as the product of self-doubt.

It may be that an elemental quality of the Contrast Tule is the described connection to its relationship with the ancient Chinese concept of the Tao, particularly the degree to which the Tule may be seen as identifying a source for what here are known as energetics of being. Deriving these views for the self can supply new reaches for places or pathways in awareness which it is the intent of this author to serve.

Such energetics of being may exist unused or used though not knowingly. When one consciously or otherwise allows the self to use such energy to derive or confirm a condemnation of the self, that energy is being misused. The emotional sense of disheartenment that may come with these occurrences is a reminder both that the motive quality of this energy exists (perhaps you were understandably unaware) and that there is a different powerfully intended and impactful way to be using such energy for your betterment and well-being. This reminder exists to tell you what that is.

Refinement. When you see these words return to and read the description of the Refinement Tule. The Lifeboat's survival-skills-based energy you may currently be using to do damage to your own concept of self is best intended by Love to be used in the more creative act of Refinement. A typically common theme in judgment is finality. Reshaping discernment is the stuff of creation in Refinement, a stuff of continual advancing movement, not finality at all. The energy you are using to condemn yourself on any terms or for any reason is better used to pick yourself up, acknowledge what you can now see to have done differently, reshape yourself by incorporating the lesson learned, and promise yourself to act newly in the next occurrence of a similar experience, event, or theme in thought. Remember that the Full Presence Tules, of which Refinement is one, identify states of being, which here are viewed as inherent and automatic normative realities operating for you, within you, in every moment, and when by choice, within your individual attentive authority.

To merely acknowledge the potential legitimacy of this thought is the beginning of making this conception a real and motive personal force in your life. To understand the distinction is to delve bright reaches of being.

When you see the simple choice to make a shift from self-judgment to creative process in Refinement, even when it may be difficult to admit the specific matter for which it had seemed so easy to condemn oneself (remember you are alone here), you are also participating in the deeply beneficial shift of human energy from a use for means of survival to a use for means of creation. In perhaps comedically strict voltaic terms, it is also a very much nicer and easier thing to do with oneself~ to see a stronger, more beneficial use for any thought or act of self-condemnation and to move away from that self-destructive practice by seeing yourself in the act of Refinement instead, and to create and advance whatever habit forms you can in such terms.

It is at first the Contrast Tule that is telling you to do this. The Refinement Tule is telling you how.

III.
Conditioning & Action

There is no battle between the intuitive self and the conscious mind. There can seem to be when an individual refuses or is so overwhelmed by fear as to be unable to face all the information available in his or her conscious mind. Sometimes it seems easier to avoid the frequent readjustments in behavior that the self-examination component of Refinement can require.

When in this state we can be bombarded with many second-hand beliefs which may contradict each other or contradict clarities you already hold or might otherwise be deriving, and which then can result in a muddled jumble of conflicting messages given to the body and the conscious mind. While this is occurring the inner self will transmit to the conscious mind insights and intuition meant to clear its sight. If you were still then to deny that support of the inner self, you might find it that you were denying or turning aside from a part of who you are.

It is a common theme for individuals to find that we may be living as the product of conditioning by our cultural experiences. The situation described above may be one product of such cultural conditioning. When we can see this, it is useful to acknowledge that to live with the conditioning of one's culture is a quite common human experience in which you are not alone. The Tules exist in large part both to aid you in noticing that conditioning along with your individual part in it, and to supply means to navigate the challenges as you train yourself in the mental strength to be a voice for truth.

If you come to notice the unmoving rigidity of your conditioned mind, you may be facing a situation you are simply not willing to currently resolve. This is an example of a circumstance to face as well as you can, and around which not to render judgment against yourself for your current unwillingness or fear. One might then call to another for help with encouragement to resolve the dilemma or face the fear.

Circumstances such as these commonly do relate to the cast of character that we hold in relation to others and each of us is free completely in all such regards to hold ourselves within or as any terms of being that we may choose. It is when our choices can knowingly do harm to another that the Refinement Tule is calling you to look again.

When this is so, a further alternative is to look at the responsible construction and accomplishment of a communication that would avert any harm done to others because of your chosen state of knowing inaction. It can be true that just such a looking, and nothing more, can supply for you an awareness of your own intent at a level adequate to help you take the leap of being required. If that looking cannot accomplish such a leap, then your personal authority would be challenging you to deliver any communications that left unsaid could do or continue the doing of emotional harm to another.

~MRM

The Cut-outs

The Cut-outs are your first available set of Tules. You can use these Cut-outs either as a guide for making your own set or by cutting them out of the book to <u>be</u> your first, if very simple, set.

They are here as a reaffirmation of the important benefits derived upon giving yourself a functional relationship with the Tules and to depict how easily that can be accomplished by allowing yourself a familiarity with the symbols.

Unlike those you would make for yourself, this set is two-dimensional. If you choose to carve your own set, remember that the Tules are intended to be audible to your hands. Carve them deep so that you can recognize each with your eyes closed.

The author created his first set by cutting a branch off a tree, cutting slices from that branch, and burning the individual images into those slices with a wood burning tool. If you follow that path, use a hand saw, carefully cutting the slices any thickness you like, making certain that the symbols, as you finally create them for yourself, following the images here, are fully intelligible to you.

However you may choose to give life to the Tules for yourself, it remains imperative to all responsible and competent use of the Tules that you complete the reading of this entire book.

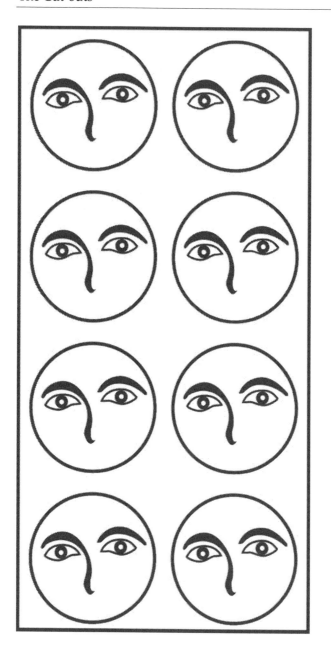

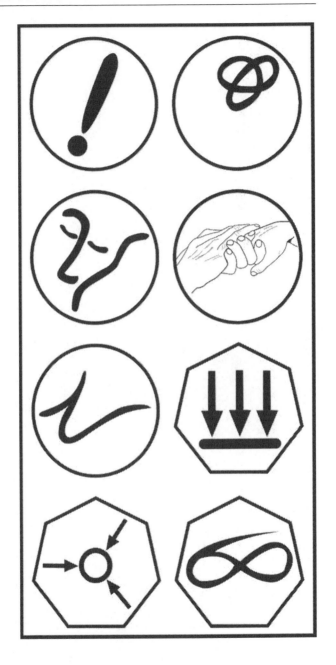

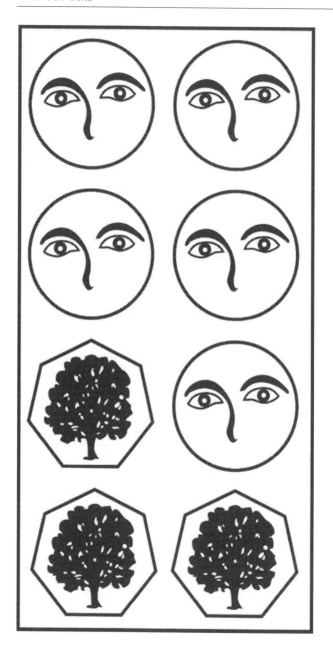

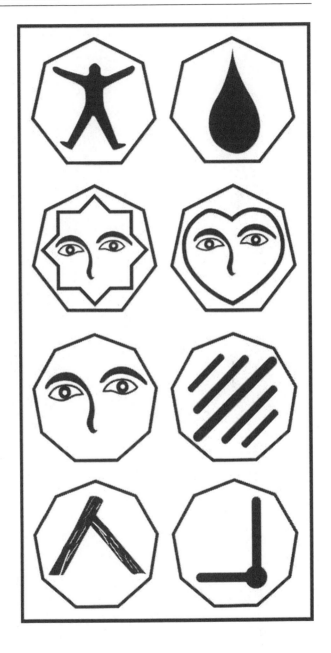

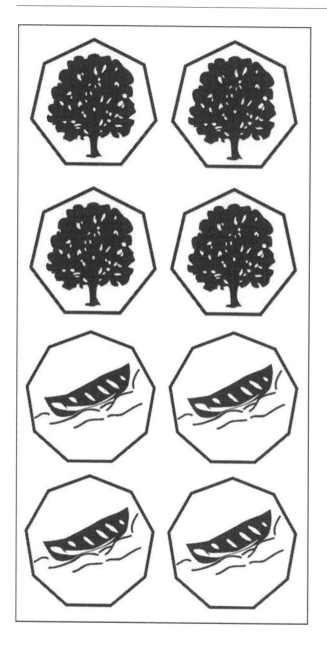

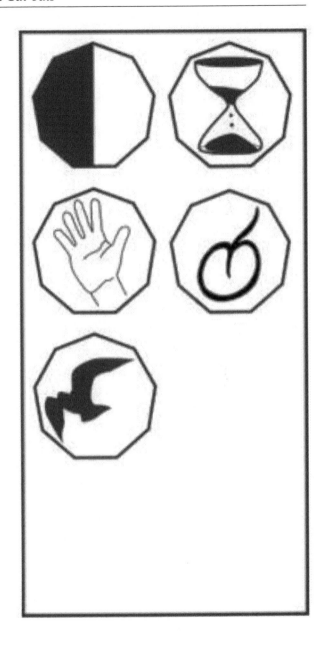

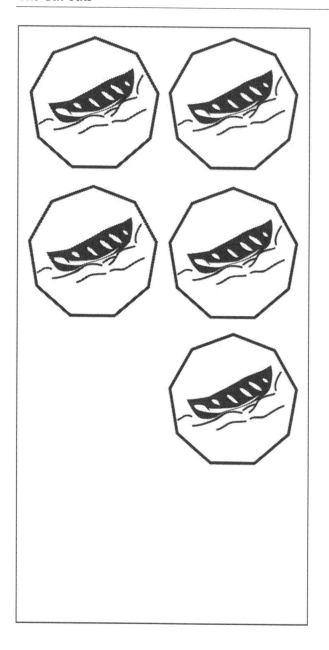

Acknowledgments

Tulcidious is visible today Thanks to the enthusiastic determination of Michael Beloved and Scott Mastrow and the firm, calm, and quiet kindness of Carol Goodwin. The artwork was accomplished in part with creative support from Ellen Witherite. Ingrid Wood, Dorothy Rankin, and Joni Steiner, all presented questions and comments that resulted in meaningful levels of additional clarity and substantive explanation. The back-cover photo of the author is the gift of R. Erik Weigand. The further essential personal acknowledgments remain innumerable.

The meanings of most words presented here, are based upon those supplied by standard English dictionaries, particularly for example, Webster's Third New International Dictionary. The word, Tulcidious, is of the author's invention and derived from the name of Tulsidas, a famous Indian poet of the seventeenth century, one among a wealth of sages throughout human history who have dedicated their lives to helping derive the always further advancement of our healthy human way.

The work itself is founded upon a private personal experience of the past and certain measures of mutual requirement as between the author and residents of the vast beyond.

The author's commitment to the use of imagery was first inspired by Shel Silverstein, his choice to think for vision by Isaac Asimov and the playwrights of the world. His curiosity around all the simplest beginnings of adult relationship was seeded through the gifts of Anthony Trollope. Werner Erhard taught the author what remains to him of determination. Patanjali Maharishi taught him how to understand human fear. The Buddha taught him that all things fit into purpose. Brian Weiss refined his thinking about looking around. Chögyam Trungpa's affirmation of the Great Eastern Rising Moon taught him Love. The lifelong inspiration of Ram Dass gently and masterfully held a truth for the author that will always be infinite.

The author's stretches in the mystical were aided by a variety of vibrational realities he found whispering through the lives of numerous gifted, beautiful people at the turn of the twenty-first century.

Infinite praise in Thanks is also found due by the author to a clarified variety of known and unknown ancients beyond sight, all of music, the miracles of poetry, and much more. His persistent dedication to the simplicity of this text has been inspired in new pertinent part by daily life in the necessary work of many expert writers even yet alive and well. Thanks is also finally due to Sue Monk Kidd, Pema Chodron, all who write with their skill, and the kind good memory of Jiddu Krishnamurti.

Thanks also for these comments from three early-version readers:
~ "Brilliant."

~ "Amazing."

~ "This is the basis of harmonious life."

And this from a late version reader on one of the shorter recitations in the Compendium:

~"You could not have written that more beautifully."